Thomas Cook

BAVARIA
including MUNICH

BY
JAMES BENTLEY,
CHRISTOPHER CATLING AND TIM LOCKE

Produced by
Thomas Cook Publishing

Written by James Bentley, Christopher Catling and Tim Locke
Updated by Barbara Rogers
Original photography by Antony Souter
Original design by Laburnum Technologies Pvt Ltd

Editing and page layout by Cambridge Publishing Management Ltd, Unit 2, Burr Elm Court, Caldecote CB3 7NU
Series Editor: Karen Beaulah

Published by Thomas Cook Publishing
A division of Thomas Cook Tour Operations Ltd
Company Registration No. 1450464 England

PO Box 227, The Thomas Cook Business Park,
Unit 18, Coningsby Road, Peterborough PE3 8SB, United Kingdom
E-mail: books@thomascook.com
www.thomascookpublishing.com
Tel: +44 (0)1733 416477

ISBN: 978-1-84157-443-1

Project Editor: Linda Bass
Production/DTP Editor: Steven Collins

Printed and bound in Italy by: Printer Trento.

Contents

KEY TO MAPS

✈ Airport   ⭐ Start of walk/tour   ✕ Restaurant

A9 Road number   1452m ▲ Mountain   ⓘ Information

🅤 U-Bahn   ⌂ Mountain hut

🅢 S-Bahn   ✝ Cross

Introduction

Bayern (Bavaria) is a rewarding region of myriad attractions; among them are such well-known sights as Oberammergau and its Passion Play, the fairytale castles of King Ludwig II – copied by Disneyland but authentic only in Bavaria – and Munich, a sophisticated centre of fashion and city of superlative works of secular and religious architecture, as well as host to the most raucously entertaining beer festival in the world.

The 1,000-m (3,280-ft) long castle at Burghausen is the longest existing in Europe and has as many as six different courtyards

Apart from its sights, Bavaria is renowned for its colourful customs. Bavarians proudly wear their exquisite woollen garments and daintily embroidered shirts and skirts complemented by leather shorts and feather-decorated felt hats. Folklore

groups entertain with traditional dancing, and the cattle that descend to the lower pastures as winter approaches are decked out in the last of the summer's flowers. In the region's walled towns and villages, festivals and pageants recall, and sometimes re-enact, stirring historical events.

Bavaria is a place where you can indulge in massive platters of food accompanied by some of the world's finest beers or, if you prefer, delicate Franconian wines. Alternatively, you can visit the region's spas in order to luxuriate in their healing waters or in restorative mud baths. For accommodation you can choose between first-class hotels in major cities and homely inns in unspoilt villages. Touring the region you will find majestic ancient churches alongside swirling rococo shrines; fortresses set over crags, and defensive castles sheltering knightly halls and opulent boudoirs for courtly ladies; and baroque palaces decorated by Austrian and Italian artists.

Those who love the wild will find a

Bavaria

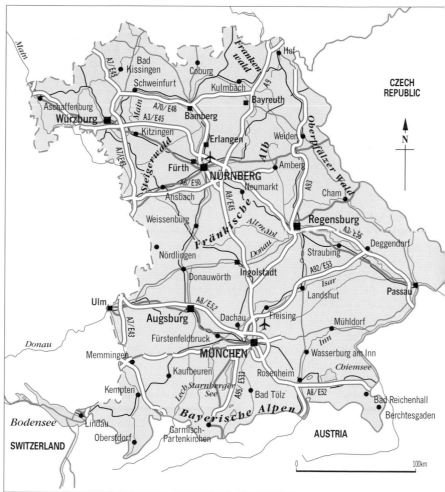

region of protected nature parks threaded by meticulously waymarked paths, of rivers that sometimes scour ravines and at other times gently meander, and of lush landscaped gardens.

For those in search of sport, Bavaria offers Olympic-class skiing facilities and numerous lakes with motor boats, rowing boats, windsurfing, water-skiing and shingled beaches from which you can swim (in designated areas) or strip naked and bronze yourself in the summer sun. Bavaria offers all this and more, making it one of the most rewarding parts of Europe to explore.

The land

Bavaria is the largest of Germany's 16 *Bundesländer* (Federal States). It covers 70,553sq km (27,240sq miles) and comprises the whole of southeastern Germany. Over half its population of some 12 million live in towns and cities (a fifth in cities of more than 100,000 inhabitants). Its capital, München (Munich), sits on a plateau between the Donau (Danube) and the Bayerische Alpen (Bavarian Alps) and is Germany's third-largest city.

Extensive forests cover more than a third of Bavaria's countryside

Mountains

Bavaria's southern borders are sheltered by the Central Alps whose peaks include Germany's highest mountain, the Zugspitze (2,963m/9,721ft), as well as the Watzmann (2,713m/8,901ft). These Alpine ranges retain snow for half the year, as do the lesser mountains of northeastern Bavaria. Elsewhere the summers are warm and the vine-clad valley of the lower Main is particularly mild, but in winter, cold weather sharply returns.

Water

Two major rivers, the Danube and the Main, cross Bavaria, linked by the Rhein-Main-Donau Canal. Bavaria is a totally landlocked state but it has numerous lakes (*see pp135–6*). Among the largest are the Chiemsee (82sq km/32sq miles, *see pp66–7*), and the Starnberger See (21km/13 miles long, up to 5km/3 miles wide and 123m/404ft at its deepest). Bavaria also includes the eastern shores of the Bodensee (Lake Constance), central Europe's third-largest lake (76km by 14km/47 miles by 9 miles), which is fed by the River Rhine

and lies on the borders of Germany, Austria and Switzerland. Among smaller lakes is the narrow Königssee (*see pp76–7*), set within the Berchtesgaden National Park (*see pp138–9*).

Forests

More than 30 per cent of Bavaria is forested. Tracts of spruce, mixed with beech and silver fir, cover the Alpine slopes. Similar woodland cloaks the low mountain ranges of the Bayerischer Wald (Bavarian Forest) in the east. Together with the adjoining National Park Böhmerwald (Bohemian Forest), in the Czech Republic, the forest parks of the Bavarian Forest form the largest forested region in Europe (*see p138*). The Bavarian Forest is divided by the Pfahl, a quartz ridge varying in height from 20m to 30m (66–98ft), that follows the Regen Valley. Northeast of this ridge is the highest peak in the Bavarian Forest, the 1,456m (4,777ft) Grosser Arber. The 63,000 ha (155,671 acres) of deciduous trees (chiefly oak and beech) in the Spessart Forest of Franconia contrast with the conifers that make up the rest of Bavaria's woodland.

The land

Geologically, Bavaria has a base of granite and laminated quartz, feldspar and mica. Sandstone underlies the northern parts, where the stone houses built by people of Frankish descent contrast with the region's half-timbered homes and farmsteads. In the limestone region east of Nürnberg (Nuremberg), the Altmühl Valley is pitted with underground caves, including the 1,200-m (3,937-ft) long Maximiliansgrotte near Burg Veldenstein.

Wheat, rye and barley are the main cereal crops, though a good quarter of the land is devoted to the hops and vines that produce Bavaria's celebrated beers and the wines of Franconia. The Hallertau in lower Bavaria is the world's largest hop-growing region. As well as this traditional agricultural base, Bavaria has a prosperous industrial sector, which employs over half the working population, and a substantial tourist trade.

Fauna

Some of the more unusual animals to survive in the Nationalpark Bayerischer Wald (Bavarian Forest National Park) are pine martens, wildcats and red squirrels, spied on by eagle owls and the shy lynx. The Hass mountains are a breeding ground for birds of prey, while wild boars roam the woods. Among the Alpine animals treasured here are the chamois, the mountain hare, salamanders, various species of rare woodpecker, and the black grouse.

Flora

Violet and yellow gentians (distilled at Berchtesgaden to make Enzian liqueur) are just two of the striking species that dot the lower slopes of the Alps. As you climb in late winter, you may see hellebores (Christmas roses) peeping out of the ground. You may admire – but are not allowed to pick – the many different species of rare Alpine plants. The locals still believe that certain plants have magical properties; kitchens in the Berchtesgaden region, for instance, are decorated with willow stems because they are believed to fend off witches.

The best way to learn about Bavaria's rich wildlife is to explore one of the region's national parks (*see pp136–9*).

Alpine gentians flower during July and August

History

1st century BC	Bavaria is inhabited by the Celts, who are increasingly subjected to harassment by the Romans and Teutons.
1 BC	Augsburg is founded and named after the Emperor Augustus.
5th century AD	Germanic tribes drive out the Romans.
7th and 8th centuries	Foreign monks convert the Bavarians to Christianity.
788	Karl der Grosse (Charlemagne) incorporates Bavaria into the Carolingian Empire.
817	Bavaria is given to Ludwig the Pious, who is succeeded by his son, Ludwig the German.
907	The Huns invade Bavaria.
955	Otto I the Great drives the Huns out of the region after the Battle of Lechfeld, near Augsburg.
1180	Frederick I Barbarossa gives Bavaria to the Count Palatine Otto von Wittelsbach, whose dynasty rules until 1918.

13th to 15th centuries	Bavaria is divided up between the members of the Wittelsbach family.
1467–1508	Duke Albert IV the Wise makes Munich his capital and in 1506 establishes the principle of primogeniture.
1545	Duke Wilhelm IV reunites the territory as one duchy.
1618–48	Thirty Years' War; Duke Maximilian I fights on the side of the Habsburgs.
18th century	Bavaria is troubled by the Wars of the Spanish Succession, Austrian Succession and the Bavarian Succession (1778–9).
1790s	After the French Revolution, Bavaria joins the anti-French coalition but is occupied by France in 1796, by Austria in 1799, and again by France in 1800.
1805	The Treaty of Pressburg allots Bavaria roughly its present territory and makes it a kingdom.
1808	Bavaria's new constitution enshrines French

	Revolutionary ideals, while abolishing serfdom. Many monasteries are secularised.
1812	Bavaria joins Russia, Britain and Austria in an alliance against Napoleon.
1818	King Maximilian I Joseph proclaims a more liberal constitution.
1848	King Ludwig I is forced to abdicate because of his affair with an Irish-born dancer, Lola Montez. King Maximilian II comes to the throne.
1870	King Ludwig II commits Bavaria to the side of Prussia in the Franco-Prussian War.
1886	Ludwig II is certified insane and the throne passes to his brother Otto, who is also considered mentally deranged. Otto's uncle, Luitpold, is declared regent and governs Bavaria until his death in 1912.
1918	Kurt Eisner leads the Bavarian Revolution at the end of World War I, and deposes King Ludwig III.
1919	Eisner's assassination in Munich leads to the 'Red Terror'. Communists seize power, but in May this is followed by the 'White Terror' unleashed by the army and the Freikorps (citizens' volunteer force). Bavaria becomes part of the Weimar Republic.
1923	Adolf Hitler's Nazi party attempts to seize power through the unsuccessful Munich Putsch.
1933–45	Hitler comes to power in 1933 and Bavaria remains a Nazi bastion until the end of World War II.
1948	Bavaria becomes a *Land* (state) of the Federal Republic of Germany.
1973	Bavaria enacts Europe's most advanced environmental legislation.
1990	German reunification.
1993	Maastricht Treaty grants individual provinces self-representation at the EU, largely due to Bavaria's insistence.
2006	Munich captures world attention by hosting some World Cup matches.

Governance

Germany is a federal republic made up of 16 separate states. Most Germans regard Bavaria as the leading champion of federalism and a bulwark of democracy. In the German Federal Council (the Bundesrat), Bavaria has six out of the 68 votes. When the German parliament decided, in 1990, that the new seat of government of the united Germany should be in Berlin, Bavaria was the first state to open an office there.

Bavarian royal crown

The local scene

Bavaria's leading political party is the Christian Social Union (the CSU or Christlich-Soziale Union), the regional equivalent of Germany's Christian Democratic Party. Its main rivals, with whom it is rarely in coalition, are the Free Democratic Party (FPD) and the Social Democratic Party (SPD). With or (mostly) without such alliances, the CSU has governed Bavaria continuously since 1946 (apart from 1954 to 1957).

Dr Edmund Stoiber was elected Bavarian Minister-President in 1993, and continues to serve in that position, as well as being Chairman of the Christian Social Union in Bavaria.

The German constitution of 1946 reorganised Bavaria as a free democratic state. Elections to the Landtag, the lower house of the Bavarian parliament, take place every four years, after which the party in office selects a minister-president and a cabinet. A counterweight to the Landtag is the Senate, made up of representatives of Bavaria's various cultural, religious, economic and social groupings.

Though Bavaria is an integral part of federal Germany, and of its central political institutions, it possesses considerable autonomy, just like the other German *Länder*. The Landtag is responsible for carrying out the decisions of central government as well as its own decrees. Each *Land* has considerable financial autonomy. In theory, this ensures that in Bavaria, as elsewhere in the federal republic, there is a close rapport between the citizens and political decision-makers.

The international stage

Bavaria has profited from being part of the third most powerful economy in the world (after the United States of America and Japan). Until it was replaced by the euro, the Deutsche Mark was the world's second reserve currency. Inevitably, Germany has become the dominant force in the European Union, of which it is a founder member.

Post-war developments

This pre-eminence has been achieved despite the almost complete destruction of German industry as a result of World War II. The former division of the country into East and West, symbolised by the Berlin Wall, was partially eased by the late Chancellor Willy Brandt, who secured a treaty in 1971 that committed both sides to friendly relations.

From the fall of the Iron Curtain, Bavaria was a leader in helping nations freed from Soviet control to establish governments and their economies.

Because of Germany's Federal system, which gives each *Land* considerable political authority along with allowing regions to preserve their distinct cultures, Bavaria has been able to initiate a number of such programmes that have been far ahead of the times.

Its post-war industrial and economic growth has included both major international companies and smaller businesses, without losing the craft trades that it has always been known for. The forward-looking Future for Bavaria Action Programme has allocated over 2.9 billion euro to be invested in scientific research, employment opportunities, social programmes, education and environmental concerns. In addition, 1.4 billion euro is being invested in the High Tech Future for Bavaria Action Programme, which will bolster Bavaria's positions in scientific research and technology, further boosting the economy and creating jobs.

But enhancing the economy has accounted for only a part of Bavaria's unique initiatives. It has taken the leadership in environmental protection, an initiative which was incorporated into its constitution. The constitutional provision stresses the state's duty to be careful stewards of soil, water, air and natural areas, and to repair damage already done. As early as 1970 the Ministry of the Environment had taken responsibility for actions that became a prototype for other governments.

In 1973 Bavaria enacted Europe's most advanced environmental legislation, and in 1976 Germany's first Academy for Environment Conservation was established with goals of limiting land use, protecting agricultural and residential lands and open space, and creating sustainable long-term planning to protect and improve soil, air and water. Plans addressed issues of clean air, noise pollution, aquifers and drinking water, long-term soil quality, and even rubbish disposal. Bavaria also led Germany in mapping natural habitats, beginning in 1974.

Responsible social welfare policies have also been a Bavarian initiative. It was the first state to adopt, in 1979, a plan for psychiatric care to provide for the mentally handicapped, later extending to such areas as alcohol treatment.

Maximilian I Joseph, first king of Bavaria, in front of Munich's Nationaltheater

Baroque and rococo

After the deprivations of the Thirty Years' War (1618–48), Bavaria experienced the flowering of a new style of architecture, inspired by Austrian and Italian masters. Using exaggerated columns, mouldings and sinuous curves, baroque architects broke up wall surfaces, creating buildings of hitherto unknown splendour – as can be seen, for example, at Enrico Zuccalli's monastery church in Ettal (see p84).

In Bavaria, the tiny village of Wessobrunn became a centre for training craftsmen in the techniques of stucco and fresco work. Among those who learned their craft here were Franz Xavier, Joseph Anton and Johann Michael Feuchtmayr, all of whom made a contribution to baroque architecture. Wessobrunn was also the birthplace of Domenikus and Johann Baptist Zimmermann, whose masterpiece is the Wieskirche, a pilgrimage church near Steingaden and a UNESCO World Heritage Site.

These craftsmen displayed astonishing virtuosity. At Prien am Chiemsee (see p67), for instance, Johann Baptist Zimmermann and his son Joseph decorated the church of Maria Himmelfahrt, creating trompe-l'oeil blue canopies out of stucco and painting the 1571 Battle of Lepanto on the ceiling.

Bavaria's finest baroque architect, Balthasar Neumann, studied in Vienna. For the Residenz at Würzburg (see p127), he built a magnificently vaulted stairway, one of the finest baroque creations in Europe. This was decorated by the Venetian artist Giovanni Battista Tiepolo with what is claimed to be the largest fresco in the world.

Originating in France, the rococo style brought yet more exuberance to Bavarian buildings. Asymmetrical flourishes, flower, shell and scroll motifs, arabesques and festoons all contributed to lavish interior decoration, to furniture and even to tableware. Silversmiths and goldsmiths produced rococo treasures. Soft pastel colours added a luminosity to walls whose rococo swirls were picked out in white and gold.

The two styles spilled over into garden design, while contemporary Bavarian composers matched the architects and landscape designers with lavish baroque and rococo music. Today, you can enjoy such music in, for example, the baroque Kloster Benediktbeuern, to the southwest of Bad Tölz.

Facing page above: cupola, Ettal's church; below: ceiling, Munich's Residenz; this page above right & below: Wallfahrtskirche Steinhausen; above left: Church of St Anne, Munich

C u l t u r e

Bavarians are exceedingly proud of their *Land*, going so far as to see themselves as a separate nation within greater Germany. The *Land* has its own blue and white flag, and its borders are announced by the slogan 'Freistaat Bayern' – the Free State of Bavaria. In fact, the self-confident image they project to the rest of the world is so strong, that many foreigners have come to see specific Bavarian traditions and costumes as being representative of Germany as a whole.

Highly distinctive Bavarian dress

Germany's southernmost state, it has long been a crossroads of trading routes through the Alps to the Mediterranean, and so the easier lifestyles and informality of southern Europe have long been part of the Bavarian culture (known as *Liberalitas Bavarica* – Bavarian freethinking).

Traditions run strong. It is not rare to see men in *Lederhosen* (leather shorts) and Alpine hats with feathers and clusters of fur called *Gamsbart* (chamois beard). Especially at festive occasions, women wear traditional full-skirted *Dirndl* dresses, often decorated in colourful embroidery.

Both men and women wear exquisitely styled green jackets and capes. Folk costumes (*Trachten*) are as prized in Bavaria as kilts in Scotland and Stetsons in Texas. The *Land* boasts some 9,000 societies dedicated to their preservation. Alongside this precious tradition, Bavaria sets itself up as the most fashion-conscious region of Germany.

At the Oktoberfest (*see pp44–5*), and at any other festival, they are apt to link arms and sing out their unofficial provincial anthem: '*In München steht ein Hofbräuhaus, Eins, Zwei, Gsuffa*' ('In Munich there's a royal brewery, one, two, drink'). They reckon that their football team, FC Bayern München, is the world's greatest. They claim that their litre mugs of beer, whose contents are supplied by about 700 independent breweries, froth more wildly than any others in Germany.

In Alpine villages just south of Munich you may hear cowbells, although they are likely to be drowned by the roar of BMWs, one of Bavaria's best-known and most important products. Jobs in the BMW factory and aerospace industry have attracted a large immigrant population to Bavaria from the former Soviet states and from eastern Germany. Immigrants make up as much as one-quarter of Bavaria's population.

To make the most of the country's attractions the Bavarians have created inventive routes such as the Romantische Strasse (Romantic Road) and the Alpenstrasse (Alpine Road).

Festivals

European Week flags, Passau

Bavaria is a region of numerous festivals, many of them commemorating local historical events or celebrating the local tipple – beer. Beginning with Munich, the following are amongst the most diverting.

Munich

Fasching, the Shrovetide carnival, begins on the Friday following 7 January, when the Fasching Princess is enthroned in the Deutsches Theater. On the Sunday before Shrove Tuesday, clowns perform in the Marienplatz, and on Shrove Tuesday itself, the stallholders of the Viktualienmarkt dance in costume, some of them dressed like the chickens they normally sell. Parties and costumed balls fill the city with revelry.

The **Starkbierzeit**, or 'Strong Beer' festival, traditionally takes place two weeks after Ash Wednesday and continues until Easter; during this time the various breweries produce beers of extra-special strength (more than 16%).

Another Munich beer festival, the **Maibock**, begins on the last Thursday in April.

The **Oktoberfest**, one of the most popular of festivals, begins at the end of September (*see pp44–5*).

The nine-day **Auerdult** takes place three times a year in Mariahilfplatz, with markets selling shoes, clothing, ceramics and glassware, junk, books and antiques. They include the **Maidult** (from the Saturday before 1 May), the **Jakobidult** (from the Saturday preceding St James's Day, 25 July) and the **Kirchweihdult**

(from the third Saturday in October) (see *www.auerdult.de*).

Augsburg

Augsburg rivals Munich in its plethora of festive events, beginning with the **Starkbierfest am Bärenbergl**, a folklore and beer festival held in March, followed by the **Frühlingsplärrer**, a folk festival around Easter.

In July, **La Piazza** is an international theatre that combines mime, circus, comedy, dance, acrobatics and slapstick.

The end of September is the time for the **Oktoberfest-Bärenbergl**, another beer festival.

Bad Tölz

St Leonhard is the patron saint of horses, and on his feast day, 6 November, the town presents its annual **Tölzer Leonhardifahrt**, a procession of decorated carts pulled by majestic horses, accompanied by citizens in traditional costumes and blaring brass bands. After the procession, in the Marktstrasse is a display of whip-cracking using old coachmen's whips.

Passau

On the Danube, Passau is known for its music, and each June and July it hosts the **European Weeks** festival, with concerts, opera, operetta recitals and oratorios held in churches, palaces and outdoor venues (*www.ew-passau.de*).

Bamberg

In the first week of July, Bamberg's **Brauerei-Nostalgiefest** (beer festival) takes place on Maximiliansplatz. This is the occasion when the city's ten private breweries vie with each other to produce their finest local speciality, the *Rauchbier* or smoked beer, so called because the barley from which it is brewed is first cured over smouldering beech wood. The **Bamberg Sandkerwa**, a festival lasting five days at the end of August, involves members of fishermen's guilds precariously jousting with long poles from boats on the River Regnitz.

Berchtesgaden

On the evening of 5 December, the night before the **feast of St Nicholas**, the menfolk of Marktschellenberg (a town just north of Berchtesgaden) dress as evil spirits for the **Butt'nmandln** festival, tying cowbells to their waists and pretending to frighten the children in their homes. These evil spirits are then defeated by St Nicholas, who comes to each house to check which children are in his gold book (giving these nuts, chocolates and oranges) and which are in his black book (in which case they are tumbled in the snow).

Coburg

In May, the **Coburger Convent** festival is devoted to the antics of the Coburg student fraternities.

The annual July **Schlossplatzfest**, set in the square in front of Schloss Ehrenburg, is a gastronomic treat organised by the leading city restaurants, with bands, actors, jugglers and dancers regaling you as you eat.

Nearby Sesslach (southwest of Coburg) hosts an **Altstadtfest** on the third weekend of August, when the streets of the upper town are filled with booths and the Marktplatz is enlisted as a beer garden.

At Rodach, northwest of Coburg, the third Saturday in December is welcomed by a **Franconian Christmas**, when the citizens parade through the town with lighted torches and hand out presents to the children in the Marktplatz.

Dinkelsbühl

Dinkelsbühl was besieged eight times during the Thirty Years' War and was finally taken by the Protestant King Gustavus Adolphus. The pleadings of its children who, in 1632, marched out to the captors bearing only flowers, persuaded the victors to spare the town. The event is remembered in the annual mid-July **Kinderzeche**, which includes performances by a 50-strong boys' band dressed in splendid red and white rococo uniforms, echoing the colours of the town's flag.

Kulmbach

The town's **beer festival**, with brass bands in traditional costume and huge barrels set up in the Marktplatz, begins on the last Saturday in July.

Landshut

In 1475, Hedwig, the 18-year-old daughter of the King of Poland, came to Landshut to marry the son of the local duke, Georg the Rich. For seven days every guesthouse and tradesman in Landshut served visitors free – at their duke's expense. The marriage was a triumph of pageantry. Since 1903, the people of Landshut have re-enacted this event, the **Landshuter Hochzeit 1475**, every third year, from the end of June to mid-July. Flags wave, flutes whistle, drums beat and dancers and jesters parade the streets in a pageant that involves over 2,000 participants dressed in early 15th-century costumes. Renaissance music plays in Burg Trausnitz and in the Residenz. The festival ends with knights in armour jousting (*also see www.landshuter-hochzeit.de*).

Nürnberg

Mid-September sees the city's **Altstadtfest**, which combines cultural and folklore events with irrepressible jazz and rock.

Regensburg

Every odd-numbered year, in June or July, Regensburg celebrates its **Bürgerfest** with folk music, copious amounts of beer, jugglers, arts and crafts displays, and theatre. In June several churches also participate in the annual **Bach week**. At the end of July, the city hosts a **jazz festival** with amateur bands from the whole of Bavaria.

Rothenburg ob der Tauber

The annual highlight of the year at Rothenburg ob der Tauber occurs over Whitsun with the celebration of the **Meistertrunk**. This pays homage to the town's Bürgermeister (Mayor) who persuaded General Tilly not to raze the

town, during the Thirty Years' War, if he managed to drink the contents of a huge flagon of wine in a single draught (*see www.meistertrunk.de/en*).

Straubing

The **Gäubodenfest** at Straubing, held during the middle two weeks of August, bids fair to rival Munich's Oktoberfest. Founded in 1812, the festival draws some 400 exhibitors from the fertile Gäuboden region whose beers are sampled by around a million visitors; as with the **Oktoberfest**, the festival is accompanied by a massive funfair. The **Agnes-Bernauer-Festspiel**, held every four years (there is one in 2007), recalls the unjust execution in 1435 of the humble peasant girl who married Duke Albrecht III.

Würzburg

Würzburg is one of the main wine-producing towns in Franconia, and it hosts several wine festivals, in particular those in the Bürgerspital, at the end of June, and the city's wine festival, at the end of September (*see www.buergerspital.de*).

One of the acts waiting to perform at Nürnberg's Altstadtfest

Impressions

The Bavarian climate is extremely variable. In Munich, for instance, July temperatures hover close to 20°C (68°F), but can rise to 35°C (95°F) for several days at a time. In January they sink to near freezing and can fall as low as −18°C (0°F). Beware, too, of the *Föhn*, a warm dry wind that sometimes blows down from the Alps and which many blame for their headaches and feelings of lethargy. On the positive side this *Föhn* wind brings with it beautifully clear air, providing a stunning view of the Alps from Munich.

THOMAS COOK'S BAVARIA

Thomas Cook's first trip to Munich took place in 1867, followed by the first Bavarian tour in 1871. A fashion for Bavarian holidays, both in summer and winter, continued well into the 1930s, with winter sports featuring in Thomas Cook brochures from the 1920s. Above all, the region became known for the Oberammergau Passion Play (*see pp90–91*), for which Thomas Cook began to arrange tours in 1880. At first the lack of hotels obliged him to arrange accommodation in private houses. He also arranged travelling interpreters to accompany his parties.

What to bring

The climate of Bavaria is at its best in the central Main Valley and to the northwest, whereas in the southeast the spa of Bad Reichenhall, for instance (*see pp62–3*), endures an annual average of 108 days of frost. Rain falls more often in the Alpine zone, yet this region also sees more sun than further north.

Depending on the season, either sandals and light clothing, or else pullovers and overcoats, are called for. In the colder months, Bavarians habitually wear felt hats, some of them decked with feathers and badges. In the winter you will see many people dressed in the beautiful heavy green woollen coats called *Lodenmantel*.

Etiquette

Bavarians shake hands when they meet. Introduced to several people at once, they shake hands with each of them. When entering a shop or a restaurant, they greet the owner with the words '*Grüss Gott*'. When leaving, it is considered impolite not to say '*Auf Wiedersehen*'.

Always address adults as *Sie*, and not as *Du* (which is reserved for children and intimate friends, though both words mean 'you'), unless, of course, specifically asked for. Convention means that you address people by their surnames, prefaced by *Herr* for a man, *Fräulein* for a girl or young woman and *Frau* for a woman (whether married or not).

If you are invited to a meal in someone's home, a bouquet of flowers is appreciated.

Wit and instant rapport

The average Bavarian has a sharp, if affectionate, wit and you should not take offence: a joke is never meant as an insult.

Markets are especially friendly and open, and the traders expect you to be the same (though they frown on people who touch vegetables before buying them). One place where you are virtually forced into instant friendship and amiable body contact is the beer garden. Especially during festivals such as the Oktoberfest, you will sit with people you have never met before and be expected to link arms while swaying to the music.

Standard church opening times
Most churches in Bavaria are open daily, 9am–5.30pm (sometimes to 6pm). In Munich the larger churches may open an hour or so earlier and close later. Churches are not open for sightseeing during church services. Admission to churches in Bavaria is usually free (exceptions are noted at the end of individual entries in this guide).

A typical Munich beer garden

Bavarians, in particular Munich's waiters and waitresses, can be a bit gruff. It takes a bit of getting used to, but you will find that a compliment to the chef (if appropriate), via the service personnel, will increase the chances of friendlier service the next time round. You will also notice that if you ask a Bavarian (or any other German for that matter) the standard question 'how are you?', they will often take it seriously and answer quite directly with the truth – not the standard 'fine thanks, how are you?'

Cultural diversity

'Wir wollen Teutsche sein und Bayern bleiben.'
'We want to be Germans and to remain Bavarians.'
KING LUDWIG I

Bavaria incorporates various groups, each with its own traditions. As well as high German, three different dialects are spoken: Old Bavarian, East Franconian and Swabian-Alemannic. Half of the population speak Old Bavarian. Next in number are the Franconians (nearly 4 million); their region, Franken (Franconia), has been

BAVARIA'S COAT OF ARMS

Some elements of the arms of the Bavarian Free State can be seen all over the world, since they are used on cans and bottles of Löwenbräu beer. The background consists of blue-and-white lozenges (or diamond shapes) superimposed with a rampant golden lion. The lion derives from the escutcheon of the Counts Palatine of the Rhine, while a rampant blue panther was formerly part of the escutcheon of the Wittelsbach family. Three black lions, in the past part of the arms of the Hohenstaufen Dukes of Swabia, also adorn the state coat of arms, while a final field, a red-and-white rake, comes from the former escutcheon of the Prince-Bishops of Würzburg. On top of the whole is a crown with five ornamental leaves, symbolising not a monarch but the sovereignty of the people of Bavaria.

The rampant lion and blue-and-white lozenges of the Bavarian flag

part of Bavaria since the early 19th century. Thirdly, Bavaria includes over 1½ million Swabians, descendants of subjects of the Hohenstaufen emperors who ruled from 1138 to 1254.

Finally, this part of Germany houses Sudeten Germans, who were exiled from Czechoslovakia in 1945. In 1962, this group was officially recognised as being 'one of the ethnic groups of Bavaria'.

Frauenkirche's steeples tower over the streets

München

Munich

The city takes its name, München, from the word for monks, referring to the small Benedictine monastic community that had been established by the River Isar in the early 9th century. The *Münchener Kindl*, or little monk, is the city emblem even today. Duke Henry the Lion built a bridge over the river and fortified the town; it then prospered as the centre of the regional salt monopoly. In 1158, Munich became the ducal residence of the powerful Wittelsbachs, later to rule Germany in 1255, and the Bavarian capital in 1503.

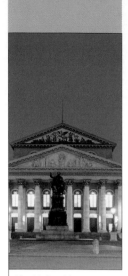

The Nationaltheater

Palaces, rococo and art

During the 17th and 18th centuries the Wittelsbachs enriched the city. Churches and two palaces were built; baroque and rococo embellishments became widespread as the city grew. Munich further expanded in the 19th century under King Ludwig I. Longing to remodel his capital on the cities of ancient Greece, he inaugurated Ludwigstrasse, which was completed in 1852. He also founded the university and endowed the city with some of its great art and antiquity collections. His successor, King Maximilian II, commissioned the architect Friedrich Bürklein to lay out Maximilianstrasse (1852–75).

City of culture, beer and greenery

Today Munich is one of the most likeable cities in Germany. It suffered heavy bombing in World War II but has resurrected itself, and you would hardly imagine what it had been through by looking at the city centre today. Overwhelmingly it is a city of elegant avenues, greenery, chic shops, church towers, monuments, fountains, classical and Jugendstil architecture; of beer gardens and beer halls; of trams in the ubiquitous Bavarian livery of blue and cream; of buskers, students, galleries and pavement cafés.

The Bavarian capital has a reputation for easy-going liberalism – its atmosphere is almost tangibly different from most of the rest of ultra-conservative Bavaria. During the Oktoberfest and the exuberant Fasching (carnival season – 7 January until Shrove Tuesday) the city really comes into its own.

Where to begin

Munich presents an embarrassment of choice: all visitors should try to explore the old city on foot, to take in a beer garden or beer hall and to stroll along the many tree-lined boulevards. The greatest museums are the Alte Pinakothek, an art collection of international importance, the Deutsches Museum and the Residenz with its remarkable treasury. If you want to sample some particularly Bavarian aspects of the city museums, go to the Bayerisches Nationalmuseum for the crib scenes, to the Stadtmuseum for the folk dancers and the puppets, to the Bavaria Filmstadt for a glimpse into the Bavarian film industry, and to the Lenbachhaus, Schackgalerie and Pinakothek der Moderne for Bavarian art. Special tickets can be purchased covering entry to all state museums. Beyond the centre, Dachau and Schloss Nymphenburg should be shortlisted on any itinerary. Three great viewpoints are from the top of the Altes Rathaus, from the Peterskirche tower and, above all, from the Olympic tower.

Getting around

The city centre is easily explored on foot. If you want to come and go as you please, you should buy a day pass (*Tageskarte*), obtainable from stations and some shops and hotels. Be sure to frank the ticket with the date by putting it into one of the machines in the stations or in the trams (but only do this once) – you are then free to use all trams, buses and S-bahn and U-bahn trains until 4am the next morning (*see transport map on pp186–7*). Unless you are going well out of the centre, get the cheaper ticket for the *Innenraum* (inner area). Also good value is the München Welcome Card, a pass that not only enables unlimited use of public transport in the city area, but also offers significant reductions on many places of interest. It is valid for either one or three days, for individuals or couples. For details contact the tourist office (*see page 51*).

The rooftops of Munich seen from one of the city's many vantage points

Munich

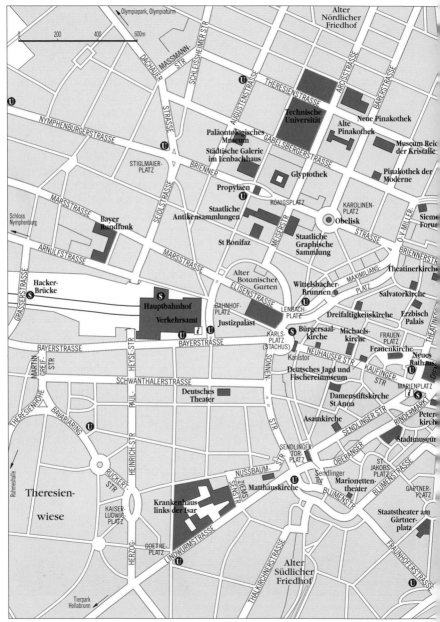

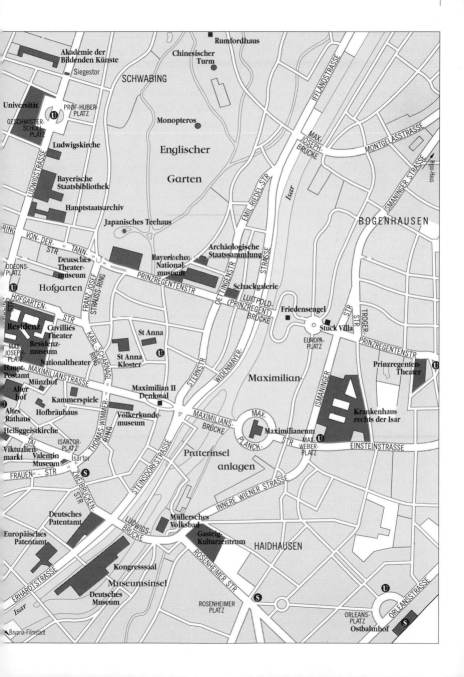

GETTING YOUR BEARINGS
Gateways

The old city was severely bombed in World War II and has been much reconstructed. The city walls have gone but four city gates survive: Karlstor, Sendlinger Tor, Isartor and the Siegestor.

A whirl of traffic skirts Karlstor in Karlsplatz, east of the area around the Hauptbahnhof, the main railway station (itself unexciting but a good bet for inexpensive accommodation). Karlsplatz, universally known as Stachus – derived from the name of Eustachius Föderl, who ran an 18th-century beer cellar here – is one of Munich's main squares, leading into the colourful pedestrian area of Neuhauser Strasse.

Neuhauser Strasse and Marienplatz

Karlstor leads into Neuhauser Strasse, an undistinguished but cheerful pedestrianised main shopping street full of buskers and street theatricals. Walk its length to the Altes Rathaus, where you are likely to hear several renditions, played with varying degrees of skill, of *Eine Kleine Nachtmusik* (arranged for string quartet, xylophone and harmonica). The Richard Strauss Brunnen (fountain) and Bürgersaal are on this street, while to the north and south respectively lie two of Munich's most renowned churches – the Frauenkirche, whose prominent twin onion-domed towers are a symbol of the city, and the astonishing Asamkirche. Near Peterskirche is the delightful Viktualienmarkt, a high-priced but high-quality food market (a great place to shop for a picnic: the Black Forest smoked hams and regional cheeses are wonderful).

Residenz, Odeonsplatz and Maximilianstrasse

Just to the north of Marienplatz lie some of the most visually appealing parts of the centre, with the huge Residenz and classical Nationaltheater abutting Max-Joseph-Platz. Close by the Residenz, the Alter Hof was the court of the ruling Wittelsbach family from 1253; its courtyard is a tree-shaded retreat.

Nearby are the Feldherrnhalle and Theatinerkirche looking on to Odeonsplatz, itself crisscrossed by students on bicycles on their way to and from the nearby university. The adjacent Hofgarten makes a pleasant retreat from the bustle. Maximilianstrasse contains many elegant and exclusive shops and galleries; eastwards it reaches the Max II Denkmal, a monument to King Maximilian II Joseph.

University area and Schwabing

Northwards Ludwigstrasse extends long and straight past the Bayerische Staatsbibliothek (Bavarian State Library) to the Siegestor; beyond is the student district of Schwabing, distinguished by a plethora of pavement cafés, wholefood restaurants, nightspots, alternative bookstores and second-hand shops (the latter to be found around Münchener Freiheit). Dress tends towards the anti-establishment and Green politics are discussed in student bars, while radical artists sell their output from street stalls.

Across the Isar

Maximilianstrasse continues as the Maximiliansbrücke over the surprisingly verdant River Isar, which flows well to the east of the city centre; the street rises to the Maximilaneum, the imposing seat of the Bavarian parliament and senate. The River Isar offers boat hire and you can stroll upstream along its banks from the Luitpoldbrücke.

This latter bridge combines with the Friedensengel, the Angel of Peace monument (erected in 1896 in memory of a quarter century of peace after the Franco-Prussian War), to create a harmonious ensemble beside the river.

Eastern suburbs

The fashionable Haidhausen harbours the Gasteig-Kulturzentrum (Gasteig Arts Centre) with its popular theatres, cinemas and the Philharmonic Hall (built in 1985). Here, too, you will find a group of picturesque 18th-century houses known as Herberghäuser and a 'French quarter'. Arabella Park is dominated by the hugely prominent and controversial Hypo-Haus with its aluminium-clad cylindrical towers, built for the Hypo Bank in 1981.

Museum quarter

The major museum quarter is north of the Hauptbahnhof, although there is another notable cluster of museums in Prinzregentenstrasse, which skirts the southern edge of the huge Englischer Garten (English Garden).

The impressive façade of the Residenz abutting Max-Joseph-Platz

Sculpture at Glyptothek

Ägyptische Kunst
(State Collection of Egyptian Art)

This absorbing and representative survey of Egyptian art was begun by the Wittelsbach family and is housed within the Residenz (*see pp46–7*). It includes statues and figures of kings and deities, religious artefacts, gold treasures from the Early, Middle and Late Dynasties, and items from the ancient Roman palace of Emperor Hadrian.
Residenz, Max-Joseph-Platz 3.
Tel: (089) 289 27630. Open: Tue–Fri 9am–5pm, Sat & Sun 10am–5pm, also Tue 7–9pm. Closed: Mon. Admission charge (Sun free). U-Bahn: 3, 4, 5 & 6 to Odeonsplatz; S-Bahn: to Marienplatz; tram: 19. Note that the museum is scheduled to relocate.

Alte Pinakothek
(Old Picture Gallery)

Opened in 1838, the Alte Pinakothek rates among the world's greatest art galleries. Originally based on a set of paintings commissioned by Duke Wilhelm IV of Bavaria in the 16th century, its resurrection from the ashes of wartime destruction has been a symbol of Munich's resilience.

Although there is too much here for a single visit, the user-friendly layout – organised by country and period – makes it easy to comprehend the scope of the collection, which concentrates on European art from the Middle Ages to the 18th century.

Among the German masters are the instantly recognisable works of Albrecht Dürer, notably *The Four Apostles (Die Vier Apostel)*, *The Baumgärtner Altar* and *Self Portrait*. One of Dürer's greatest contemporaries was Matthias Grünewald: see, for example, his picture *The Mocking of Christ (Verspottung Christi)*. The Dutch and Flemish collection features a virtually unrivalled set of paintings by Peter Paul Rubens, including the *Self-portrait with his Wife in the Arbor* and the huge *Great Last Judgement*. Pieter Brueghel's *Fool's Paradise* was painted in 1567 to rally popular support against the Spanish military occupation of the Netherlands.

Italian representation is succinct but choice, with a haunting trio of Madonna portraits by Raphael, a *pietà* by Botticelli, a *Virgin and Child* (controversially restored) by Leonardo da Vinci, and a superb altarpiece by Tiepolo among others. French masterpieces include the idealised Arcadian landscapes of Claude Lorrain and Nicolas Poussin. *See also the* Neue Pinakothek (*p40*).

Barerstrasse 27 (enter from
Theresienstrasse). Tel: (089) 238 05216;
www.altepinakothek.de.
Open: Tue–Sun 10am–5pm, also Tue
5–8pm. Closed: Mon.
Admission charge (Sun free).
U-Bahn: 2 & 8 to Königsplatz;
tram: 27 to Pinakothek; bus: 154.

Antikensammlungen (State Collection of Classical Art) and Glyptothek

Both museums owe their provenance to
Ludwig I who, during the early 19th
century, toured the sites of the ancient
world seeking out items for the
collections. The result is a rich and eye-
catching collection of classical art.
Highlights of the Antikensammlungen
are the Etruscan jewellery and the
superb Greek decorative vases and urns.

Across the square the cool, classical
architecture of Leo von Klenze's
Glyptothek is an apt purpose-built
setting for a museum devoted to
statuary and sculpture; the highlight is
the pediment from the Aphaia Temple
in Aegina (505–485 BC). Also not to be

The Alte Pinakothek (Old Picture Gallery) is one
of the best art galleries in the world

missed is the *Barberini Faun.*
Königsplatz 1. Tel: (089) 599 88830;
www.antike-am-koenigsplatz.mwn.de
(Antikensammlungen) and (089) 286
100; www.glyptothek.de (Glyptothek).
Antikensammlungen open: Tue &
Thur–Sun 10am–5pm, Wed 10am–8pm.
Closed: Mon. Glyptothek open: Tue, Wed
& Fri–Sun 10am–5pm, Thur 10am–8pm.
Closed: Mon. Admission charge, except
Sun & holidays.
U-Bahn: 2 & 8 to Königsplatz; tram: 27
to Karolinenplatz.

Archäologische Staatssammlung (State Archaeological Collection)

This compact modern building near the
Englischer Garten yields plenty of
surprises. The appealingly exhibited
collection covers aspects of early human
activity in Bavaria, from the Stone Age
to the early Middle Ages.
Lerchenfeldstrasse 2. Tel: (089) 211 2402;
www.archaeologie-bayeth.de. Open:
Tue–Sun 9am–4.30pm. Closed: Mon.
Admission charge. U-Bahn: 4 & 5 to
Lehel; tram: 17; bus: 100.

Dürer's famous work, *Die Vier Apostel*

Asamkirche (Asam Church)

This glorious rococo building is named after its brilliant architects, the brothers Ägid Quirin Asam (1692–1750) and Cosmas Damian Asam (1686–1739). They built it as a private chapel (1733–46), but the citizens of Munich liked it so much that the brothers agreed to let them use it as a parish church. Both men had studied baroque architecture in Rome. As well as being an architect, Ägid Quirin was a brilliant sculptor, while Cosmas Damian put his talents above all into frescoes.

The entrance is flanked by naturalistically carved lumps of jagged bedrock. St Johann Nepomuk (to whom the church is dedicated) is sculpted on the façade, along with portrait medallions of Pope Benedict XIII and Bishop Johaan Theodor of Freising.

The undisputed genius of the Asam brothers is revealed beyond the oval-shaped entrance, with its swirling confessionals. Here, the confessional on the right is adorned with two white and winged skulls. One gruesomely depicts sinfulness and is entwined with a golden snake; the other, as its golden laurel wreath indicates, represents saintliness.

The church opens out into a dazzling display of elliptical curves and structural irregularity. Golden stucco garlands and a double balcony lead the view to the choir, centring on a glass reliquary containing a bone and a wax effigy of St Johann Nepomuk. The ceiling fresco above depicts scenes from his life and pilgrims visiting his tomb.

The gallery altar above the tabernacle is set amidst wildly twisting columns

The entrance to the Asamkirche. . .

and flanked by angels sculpted by Ignaz Günther in 1767, all lit by a window around which gilded stucco represents the rays of the sun. Portraits of the Asam brothers flank the high altar (Ägid Quirin on the left and Cosmas Damian on the right). Dominating the whole east end is the Throne of Grace, the work of Ägid Quirin, depicting God the Father presenting his crucified Son to the world.

At Sendlinger Strasse 61, next door to the Asamkirche, is the home that Ägid Quirin Asam built for himself, its façade a deliciously stuccoed confection featuring allegorical figures drawn from classical mythology and the Bible, the whole scene crowned with a figure of the Virgin on a crescent moon. From here, through a secret window, the architect would look into his own church. Ägid also designed the presbytery on the other side of the Asamkirche, which was completed only after his death.

Sendlinger Strasse 61 & 62.
Open: daily 8am–5.30pm.
U-Bahn: 2, 6, 7, 8 to Sendlinger Tor; bus:
52, 152 to Sendlinger Tor.

'Bavaria' and the Ruhmeshalle

Here is a massive and unmistakeable statement of Bavarian patriotism. Built on a ridge above the Theresienwiese (site of the Oktoberfest – *see pp44–5*), Leopold von Klenze's classical Ruhmeshalle (Hall of Fame) is overshadowed by the colossal bronze statue of *Bavaria*, cast in 1850 to the design of Ludwig Schwanthaler. Inside the Doric-style Ruhmeshalle are busts of several eminent Bavarians. *Bavaria*, who stands 18m (59ft) high and weighs 78 tonnes, is dressed in a bearskin and accompanied by a pet lion. Inside her, 130 steps lead up to the head, through whose empty eye sockets you can survey the city and the Theresienwiese.

Theresienhöhe 16. Tel: (089) 290 671.
Open: (1 Apr–15 Oct) daily 9am–6pm,
also during Oktoberfest 9am–8pm.
Closed: 16 Oct–Mar. Admission charge.
U-Bahn: 4 & 5 to Theresienhöhe;
bus: 62 & 66 to Theresienhöhe.

. . . and the lavishly decorated and gilded interior

Bavaria Filmstadt

Munich's 'Film City', the largest studio complex in Europe, has been producing celebrated movies since 1919. Even before then Munich was a noted film centre. The film pioneer Karl Valentin (*see pp50–51*) rivalled the early Chaplin. In the 1920s, the young Alfred Hitchcock sharpened his directorial skills in Munich with his first two films, *Irrgarten der Leidenschaft* (*The Pleasure Garden*) and *Bergadler* (*The Mountain Eagle*). Though big budget films are still made here, the emphasis these days is on television productions.

During summer, you can tour the studios on a little train known as the Filmexpress. The tour includes special-effects shows put on by stuntmen and actors who impersonate famous film stars. Various secrets of the filmmaker's art are revealed, and historic artefacts (such as the U-boat from the celebrated film *Das Boot – The Boat*) are on display. You can also wander on foot, exploring, for example, the model streets of Berlin built for Ingmar Bergman's film *The Serpent's Egg*.
*Bavariafilmplatz 7, Geiselgasteig.
Tel: (089) 6499 2300. Open: daily,
1 Mar–6 Nov 9am–4pm, 7 Nov–Feb
10am–3pm. Admission charge.
Tram: 25 to Bavariafilmplatz.*

Bayerisches Nationalmuseum (Bavarian National Museum)

If you only have time for one museum in Munich and want to see something quintessentially Bavarian, this is the obvious one to visit. Arranged on three floors, this is an all-embracing arts and crafts collection, including painted

Light and airy rococo work in the splendid Bürgersaalkirche

peasant furniture (an entire set of rooms from the Schliersee has been trans-planted here), some magnificent wood-carvings by Tilman Riemenschneider, Nymphenburg porcelain, clocks, textiles, folk art and costumes. In the basement is a huge and wonderful collection of crib scenes, one by Jakob Sandtner (1572) depicting Munich at the time, another representing Bethlehem, envisaged in 1800 in grandiose classical style. Some of the tableaux show a considerable sense of humour.
*Prinzregentenstrasse 3.
Tel: (089) 211 2401; www.bayerisches-nationalmuseum.de. Open: Tue–Sun
10am–5pm, also Thur 10am–8pm.
Closed: Mon. Admission charge (except*

Sun & holidays). U-Bahn: 4 & 5 to Lehel; tram: 17 to Nationalmuseum; bus: 53.

BMW Museum

Close to the Olympiapark, the high-tech home of BMW (Bavarian Motor Works) is clearly identifiable – the skyscraper consists of a quartet of aluminium cylinders placed together like a four-leafed clover. The museum attached to the headquarters of this prestigious company is in a newly renovated space, and takes visitors on a time-trip from the past to the future. For nostalgia lovers there are plenty of classic cars and other reminders of the romantic motoring style of yesteryear.
Petuelring 130. Tel: (089) 3822 3307.
Open: daily 10am–8pm. Admission charge.
U-Bahn: 3; buses: 36, 43, 81, 136 & 184 to Olympiazentrum; tram: 27 to Petuelring.

Bürgersaalkirche

This unmissable baroque and rococo church of 1710 was built as an assembly hall for the Marian confraternity, an order dedicated to the Virgin Mary. In its crypt is the grave of Father Rupert Mayer, who died in the Sachsenhausen concentration camp in 1945 because of his opposition to the Nazis.

Upstairs is the church. Halfway up the left-hand stairway, the Virgin is represented sheltering the faithful under her cloak. Under the organ console is a guardian angel in flowing robes, pointing to heavenwards and tenderly leading a child by the hand. Sculpted by Ignaz Günther in 1763, the angel displays a slender right leg, the infant a chubby left one. Other paintings depict the major pilgrimage sites of Bavaria. Over the high altar is a splendid 1710 relief of the *Annunciation* by Andreas Faistenberger.
Neuhauser Strasse 48.
Open: 9am–5.30pm.
U-Bahn: 4 & 5; S-Bahn: 1–8 to Karlsplatz/Stachus; trams: 18, 19, 20, 25 & 27.

The baroque façade of the Bavarian National Museum

A bronze boar greets visitors to the German Hunting and Fishing Museum

Deutsches Jagd und Fischereimuseum (German Hunting and Fishing Museum)

Housed in the former church of an Augustinian monastery, this is one of the city's quirkier museums, based on a theme that is a major facet of Bavarian folk culture. It is not a place for stuffed-animal-phobics – mounted deer heads line both walls and there are dioramas of animals in mock-ups of their habitats – but the 17th- and 18th-century hunting sledges are charming and the displays also include paintings and the world's largest collection of fish-hooks! Locals will wryly point out the Wolpertinger among the stuffed exhibits – a truly legendary zoological curiosity, not unrelated to the red herring.
Neuhauser Strasse 2. Tel: (089) 220 522; www.jagd-fischerei-museum.de.
Open: daily 9.30am–5pm (Thur until 9pm). Admission charge. U-Bahn: 3 or 6; S-Bahn: to Marienplatz; trams: 18 & 27 to Karlsplatz/Stachus.

Deutsches Museum (German Museum)

This is arguably the world leader among science and technology museums and it is the most visited museum in the city. A timetable posted at the entrance hall lists the numerous demonstrations and films taking place each day, and it is worth planning your visit around this (in any event you should devote a whole day to the museum). The exhibits range from the obviously technical and educational – such as do-it-yourself chemistry experiments and models of hydraulic systems – to areas of much more mainstream appeal. (Many of the captions for these are in German only, but detailed guidebooks in other languages are available at the entrance.) The museum is a universal hit with children, particularly older ones, and both scientific and non-scientific adults will find plenty of interest. The presentation is admirable, with arrays of buttons to press and gadgets to try out, and the displays include reconstructions of the prehistoric caves at Lascaux, Galileo's study and the interior of a coal mine. You can also gaze at the night sky in the planetarium (or the real thing from the observatory telescope) and explore a 19th-century sailing ship as well as numerous historic cars and aeroplanes. The shop is excellent for unusual souvenirs.
Museumsinsel 1. Tel: (089) 21791; www.deutsches-museum.de. Open: daily 9am–5pm. Admission charge.
U-Bahn: 1 & 2 to Fraunhoferstrasse; S-Bahn: to Isartorplatz; trams: 18 to Deutsches Museum, 17 to Isartor.

Deutsches Theatermuseum

This museum pays homage to Munich's prominence as a theatrical base through exhibitions of stage designs, costumes, stage props and theatrical memorabilia.
Galeriestrasse 4a & 6. Tel: (089) 210 6910. Open: (special exhibitions, there are no permanent displays) Tue–Sun 10am–4pm. Closed: Mon. Admission charge except Sun & public holidays. U-Bahn: to Odeonsplatz.

Dreifaltigkeitskirche

Holy Trinity Church was built in 1718, in the Italian baroque style for the Carmelite order of nuns, after a holy woman prophesied disaster for the city unless the Holy Trinity were specially honoured (curiously enough, the church escaped war damage). The architects were Johann Georg Ettenhofer and his colleague Enrico Zuccalli, but the plans they followed were drawn up by Giovanni Antonio Viscardi. Its frescoes, early work by Cosmas Damian Asam, depict the Father, Son and Holy Spirit in glory, while the stucco work is by Johann Georg Bader. The tabernacle on the high altar by Johann Baptist Straub is superb. Another altar, to the right of the high altar, has sculptures of St John and St Paul made in the 1720s by Andreas Faistenberger.
Pacellistrasse 6. Open: 9am–5.30pm. U-Bahn: 4 & 5; S-Bahn: to Karlsplatz/ Stachus; tram: 19.

Müllersches Volksbad

This admirably preserved public swimming bath, with its curvaceous domed ceiling and original lamp fittings, is a supreme example of Jugendstil (Art Nouveau) architecture (built 1897–1901) located on the east bank of the Isar by the Ludwigs-brücke (just north of the Deutsches Museum).

Leading the world's science and technology museums – the Deutsches Museum

Englischer Garten (English Garden)
The city's breathing space

This garden is, in fact, one of the world's largest city parks, extending for some 5km (3 miles) and covering 373 ha (922 acres). The remarkably countrified park is a great weekend retreat for picnickers, families and sunbathers – be prepared for the fact that Munich's citizens have a liberal attitude towards nudity and think nothing of stripping off to sunbathe. The grass grows long and unkempt, speckled yellow by dandelions; it all looks like parkland somewhat gone to seed, but its informality is part of its charm.

The informally landscaped glades of the Englischer Garten

English origins

Munich owes its English Garden to Benjamin Thompson, an American-born soldier who entered the service of the Elector Karl Theodor in 1798 and speedily reformed the Bavarian army, making numerous contributions in fields as diverse as agriculture and provision for the poor. Ennobled in 1792, he took the name Count Rumford. In 1789, he persuaded the elector to transform the marsh north of the Residenz into a park, following the pattern of 18th-century Romantic English gardens – man imitating and improving upon nature.

Its Chinesischer Turm (Chinese Tower), built in 1789 and modelled on the Pagoda in London's Kew Gardens, is today surrounded by a very popular beer garden where, on Sundays, Bavarian oompah bands are often to be heard in full swing. The Rumfordhaus (1791) was built to resemble an English colonial officer's summerhouse. Others added to the charms of the

English Garden, particularly the landscape gardener Ludwig von Sckell who, in 1803, softened the 'military' aspect of the original setting. The Monopteros, a rotunda erected by Leo von Klenze in 1837 on an artificial hill, offers a fine panorama over the garden and the neighbouring Munich skyline, taking in Ludwigskirche, the dome, and cupolas of the Theatinerkirche and the cathedral. The garden is dotted with statues of its illustrious creators, such as Elector Karl Theodor, Count Rumford and von Sckell.

Something for everyone

Several streams flow through the garden. A refreshing spot is the 'Seehaus' restaurant, which overlooks the Kleinhesseloher See, on which glide swans, ducks and geese. The garden is largely traffic free, save for a few buses and cyclists and some horse-drawn carriages catering for tourists. One intriguing innovation is a tree trail which starts at the bus stop near the Chinese Tower; the trees are identified with little plaques giving their names in German and Latin. The Japanisches

Teehaus hosts Japanese tea ceremonies in the afternoons on the second and fourth weekend of each month between April and October (book in advance, *tel: (089) 224 319*).

Open: sunrise–sunset. From the centre of Munich take U-Bahn 3 & 6 to either Universität or Münchner Freiheit or tram 17 or bus 100 to Nationalmuseum.

Frauenkirche (Munich Cathedral)

The twin onion-domed spires of Munich's late-Gothic cathedral have become one of the symbols of the city. The vast cathedral was designed by Jörg von Halspach and built between 1468 and 1488, while the towers were finished in 1524. In 1772 Ignaz Günther redesigned the main entrance and the four side portals.

Inside, its treasures include 15th- and 16th-century stained glass, in particular glass of 1493 in the choir by Peter Hemmel von Andlau of Strasbourg. In the choir there are busts of prophets and saints brilliantly carved by Ernst Grasser and his pupils in 1502. Other masterpieces are bronze statues of Dukes Albrecht V and Wilhelm IV, sculpted by Dionys Frey in 1619. In the south aisle stands the magnificent tomb of Emperor Ludwig the Bavarian (not finished till 1622, though he died in 1347).

Frauenplatz 1. Open: 9am–5.30pm. A lift takes you up the south tower (open: Apr–Oct daily, except Sun & holidays 10am–5pm). U-Bahn: 3 & 6; S-Bahn: to Marienplatz; tram: 19.

Glyptothek

See Antikensammlungen, *p29.*

Hofbräuhaus

The best-known beer hall in Munich was founded in 1589 by Duke Wilhelm V partly to appease his fastidious courtiers, who disliked the local beer, and partly to save the great cost of importing their preferred brew from the north German town of Einbeck. Knowing that it was not enough just to cut costs by building a brewery right next to his court, he also made sure he hired a brewer who knew his job. The new brew became so famous that when the invading Swedes arrived at Munich in 1632, they demanded it (and were given 60,000 litres/13,198 gallons). Bavarian bands in full swing set the tone today. The beer hall is decidedly jolly, but touristy – the local people tend to go elsewhere.

> **The Devil's Footprint**
> A celebrated fable relates that the cathedral architect made a pact with the Devil, who supplied funds on condition that the building would have no visible windows. On completing his work, the crafty architect took the Devil to a point where no window was in view – the Devil stamped his foot in rage and departed, leaving the mark you can see to this day.

Peace and colour in the Englischer Garten

Michaelskirche has Europe's widest vault, outside of Rome

Lenbachhaus

The City Art Gallery is housed in this elegant Italianate villa, built between 1887 and 1891 for Franz von Lenbach (1836–1904), the most fashionable Bavarian painter of his day. Lenbach's living quarters have been faithfully preserved along with several of his paintings. Elsewhere the museum is devoted to German art from the Middle Ages and is particularly strong on *fin de siècle* artists of the Jugendstil and the Blauer Reiter schools (*see box*). The wings of the house enclose a formal Italian garden adorned with sculpture.
Luisenstrasse 33.
Tel: (089) 2333 2000;
www.lenbachhaus.de.
Open: Tue–Sun 10am–6pm.
Closed: Mon. Admission
charge. U-Bahn: 2 & 8 to
Königsplatz; tram: 27 to
Karolinenplatz & also 20/21
to Stiglmaierplatz.

Michaelskirche

St Michael's is a Jesuit church, built between 1583 and 1597 in the Renaissance style and later partly baroque. On the façade is an eye-catching statue of St Michael the Archangel slaying the dragon. Inside, mighty pillars support the vault which is the second largest in Europe after that of St Peter's in Rome. Look out for an ethereal angel, sculpted by Hubert Gerhard in 1596 to guard the font. In 1587, to enhance the high altar, Christoph Schwarz painted the Archangel Michael thrusting Lucifer from heaven.

Some 30 members of the Wittelsbach dynasty, including Wilhelm V who paid for this church, are buried in the Princes' Crypt beneath the choir.
Neuhauser Strasse 52.

Open: daily 8am–7pm. U-Bahn: 4 & 5;
S-Bahn: to Karlsplatz/Stachus;
trams: 18, 19, 20, 25 & 27.

Museum Reich der Kristalle
(Kingdom of Crystals Museum)

The 'Reich der Kristalle' is that part of
the Mineralogische Staatssammlung
(State Collection of Mineralogy) open
to the public. This worldwide collection
of minerals includes many rarities.
Theresienstrasse 41. Tel: (089) 2394 4312
www.lrzmuenchen.de. Open: Tue–Fri

1–5pm, Sat & Sun 1–6pm. Closed: Mon.
Admission charge. U-Bahn: 3, 4, 5 or 6 to
Odeonsplatz & also 2 to Theresienstrasse.

Münzhof (Mint Court)

The Münzhof has an exquisite
Renaissance courtyard of 1567. From
1809 to 1983, it served as the Bavarian
state mint, hence its name.
Hofgraben 4. Open: Mon–Fri 8am–4pm.
Closed: weekends. Free admission.
U-Bahn: 3, 4, 5 & 6 to Odeonsplatz;
tram: 19 to Nationaltheater.

The sculpture-filled formal garden of the Lenbachhaus

Nationaltheater

Munich's National Theatre was built by Karl von Fischer between 1811 and 1818, on the site of a Franciscan monastery. Though damaged by fire in 1823, and by bombs in 1943, it has been rebuilt much as it was, a neo-Grecian edifice with a colonnade rising to a pediment whose modern sculptures (by G Brenninger, 1972) represent Apollo and the Muses. All this is topped by a 19th-century mosaic by Leo Schwanthaler featuring Pegasus.

Max-Joseph-Platz 2. Tel: (089) 2185 1920. For information and online bookings visit www.bayerische.staatsoper.de. Guided tours: most days from 2pm. Tickets for the Bavarian State Opera from the main entrance at Max-Joseph-Platz. The ticket office opens for evening sales one hour before the shows begin.

U-Bahn: 3 & 6 to Odeonsplatz or Marienplatz; S-Bahn: to Marienplatz; tram: 19 to Nationaltheater.

Neue Pinakothek (New Picture Gallery)

Founded by Ludwig I in 1846, this gallery was rebuilt after the devastating World War II bombing and only reopened in 1981. The art exhibits follow on, chronologically, from those of the Alte Pinakothek (Old Picture Gallery – *see pp28–9*) and date to the period from the late 18th century up to the 1920s. Most of the work is Bavarian art by the likes of Gustav Klimt, Egon Schiele and Carl Spitzweg, but other major European artists are here too – Gainsborough, Turner and the major French Impressionists among them.

Barerstrasse 29. Tel: (089) 2380 5195; www.neuepinakothek.de.

Open: Mon, Wed–Sun 10am–5pm (Wed until 10pm). Closed: Tue. Admission charge, except Sun & holidays.

U-Bahn: 2 & 8 to Theresienstrasse; tram: 27 to Pinakothek; bus: 53.

The Nationaltheater is a remarkable transformation from an early 19th-century Franciscan monastery

Neues Rathaus (New Town Hall)

Marienplatz is dominated by the somewhat sinister-looking neo-Gothic Neues Rathaus (1867–1908). Every visitor must experience the Glockenspiel, whose 43 bells play a 15-minute carillon at 11am (and from May until October also at noon and 5pm). As the bells peal out their tune, 32 mechanical figures, including musicians, knights and coopers, first re-enact the festivities of the marriage of Duke Wilhelm V to Renate von Lothringen in 1568, then they do a Coopers' Dance, which was first performed in 1517 because it was believed to be a way of averting the plague. You can also climb up the 85-m (279-ft) high tower. Perched on top is the *Münchner Kindl* (the little monk from whom Munich derives its name). There is a fine aerial view of the old city from the tower, but if the queues put you off, try the less-frequented Peterskirche instead (*see p43*), where the tower offers more or less the same panorama.

The marble column at the centre of Marienplatz was erected by Elector Maximilian I in 1638 to carry a statue of the Virgin Mary (sculpted by Hubert Gerhardt around 1490).

The same square also houses the Altes Rathaus (Old Town Hall), which stood here from 1345, was in part rebuilt by Jörg von Halspach in the 15th century and was severely damaged in World War II; this tragedy was followed by a fine reconstruction of the medieval Gothic building. Its tower now houses the Spielzeug Museum (*see p48*). *Marienplatz. Rathaus tower open: May–Oct, Mon–Thur 9am–4pm,*

The entertaining Glockenspiel high on the tower of the Neues Rathaus

Fri 9am–1pm, Sat, Sun & holidays 9am–7pm. U-Bahn: 3 & 6; S-Bahn: to Marienplatz; bus: 52.

Olympiapark

Built for the 20th Summer Olympics, held in 1972, this park is neat and compact, and dominated by the huge architecture of the stadium and the 28-m (92-ft) high television tower. There is plenty to see and do even when the Olympic swimming pool is out of action. You can, for example, visit the Olympiastadion (Olympic Stadium), a curious tent-like structure of steel netting and acrylic panels. This is the stadium used by Bayern-München, one of Germany's most successful football teams, when it is playing at home. The surrounding park is also very popular with cyclists, joggers, roller-skaters and casual strollers. Boats can be hired on the lakes.

The panorama from the 290-m (950-ft) Olympiaturm (Olympic Tower) is one of the sights of Bavaria. Viewed from here, the city shrinks into map-like form; the prominent cylinders of the BMW tower stand close by, resembling a gigantic set of engine pistons, gleaming metallically in the sunshine; beyond the fertile green plain south of Munich, the great chain of the Alps can be seen on a clear day – they look surprisingly near.

At night, the tower gives a lovely view of the city.

The sports facilities in the park are available for public use. These include a skating rink, swimming hall (with sauna, solarium and sunbathing area), tennis courts, bowling alley, and fitness and recreation centres. Restaurants are situated in the revolving platform halfway up the Olympic Tower. The Olympic Hall is a favoured venue for concerts. The ill-fated Olympic Village, where Israeli athletes were killed in the 1972 Olympics in a shoot-out after being taken hostage by Palestinian terrorists, serves as lodgings for

Dramatic tent-like structures grace the lakeside in the Olympiapark

university students, although most of the flats are now privately owned.
Olympiapark Visitor Service
tel: (089) 306 72414; www.olympiapark-
muenchen.de. Olympiaturm open: Mon–
Sun 9am–midnight. Olympiastadion
open: daily 9am–4.30pm. Sightseeing
tours: Apr–Oct, daily at 2pm.
U-Bahn: 3 to Olympiazentrum.

Paläontologisches Museum (State Palaeontology Collection)

This astonishing fossil and bone collection is more interesting than it may sound. On display are the spooky skeletal remains of the likes of sabre-toothed tigers and massive reindeer, along with curiously beautiful fossilised plants.
Richard-Wagner-Strasse 10.
Tel: (089) 2180 6630. Open: Mon–Thur
8am–4pm, Fri 8am–2pm, first Sun in the
month 10am–4pm. Free admission.
U-Bahn: 2 to Königsplatz.

Peterskirche (St Peter's Church)

Munich's oldest parish church was transformed in the 17th and 18th centuries when it was decorated by some of Bavaria's finest craftsmen and architects. It is also crammed with masterpieces of religious art, including a 20-m (66-ft) tall altar from 1730, designed by Nikolaus Stuber, featuring a statue of St Peter carved by Erasmus Grasser in 1492; statues of the four Doctors of the Church sculpted by Ägid Quirin Asam in 1732; and side panels painted by Jan Polack in 1517. The Bavarian tradition of preserving saints intact and on full display is bizarrely illustrated by the presence here of the skeleton of Munditia, the patron saint of

The Renaissance tower of Peterskirche offers panoramic views of the city

single women, wearing a bejewelled shroud and holding a quill pen.
Rindermarkt 1. Open: 9am–5.30pm.
U-Bahn: 3 & 6; S-Bahn: to Marienplatz;
bus: 52.

You can view the city from the Renaissance tower of Peterskirche (*open: Mon–Sat 9am–6pm, Sun 10am–6pm*). From this tower, New Year is welcomed in by trumpets.

In 1810, the marriage of Crown Prince Ludwig of Bavaria to Princess Therese von Sachsen-Hildburghausen was celebrated with horse racing in a huge meadow, which was thenceforth named the Theresienwiese in honour of the bride. Crowds of Bavarians cheered the couple. So delighted were the participants that they decided to celebrate the event year after year.

Thus began the city's famous Oktoberfest, which (in spite of its name) begins on the penultimate Saturday in September, ending on the first Sunday in October. During that time some 6 million visitors will drink a copious 5 million litres (1.1 million gallons) of beer. They do so in massive tents set up by the major breweries. They will also

consume over 300,000 pork sausages, 600,000 barbecued chickens, more than 60,000 roast pork knuckles, and an unquantifiable number of grilled fish (known as *Steckerlfische*).

Alongside the beer tents, the Theresienwiese becomes a huge fairground, with swings and roundabouts, bumper cars, roller-coasters and a giant Ferris wheel. From the decorations of the beer tents and the dress of the waitresses to the brass-band players in their Bavarian costume, the Oktoberfest, despite its international popularity, remains a quintessentially Bavarian festival.

It begins with a costume parade through the crowd-filled streets of the old city, followed by a procession of decorated horse-drawn beer carts. The opening ceremony takes place on Theresienwiese when the Bürgermeister of Munich taps open the first barrel. As he does so, he cries, in the local dialect *'Ozapft is!'* ('It's open!') to declare the Oktoberfest open.

Munich's beer is rightly celebrated as among the best in the world. Beer lovers come from all over the world for Munich's Oktoberfest

Residenz

This huge baroque palace in the heart of the city demands stamina to be seen in its entirety; different portions are opened in the morning and afternoon. Although bombed to a rubble in the last war, it has been extensively and faithfully restored. The palace is really several museums in one: the Residenz itself, the Schatzkammer (Treasury), the Cuvilliés Theater, plus the Ägyptische Kunst (Egyptian Collection – *see p28*), and the Staatliche Münzsammlung (State Coin Collection – *see p48*).

Ornate sculptures grace one of the many gateways to the Residenz

History

In 1385, the Wittelsbach family decided to build themselves a new palace in Munich. Eventually no fewer than eight different buildings clustered together to form their Residenz, the finest of these undoubtedly being François Cuvilliés' rococo theatre of 1753, run a close second by the so-called 'Rich Rooms' built in the early 18th century. Next, King Ludwig I commissioned Leopold von Klenze to build the Königsbau (King's Building) in 1826–35, which is modelled on the Pitti Palace in Florence. Von Klenze also designed the Festsaalbau (Festival Hall Building) of the royal Residenz. These buildings are matched by the magnificent vaulted Antiquarium (begun 1568), built to house the ducal art collection and transformed into a Festsaal (Dance Hall) by Friedrich Sustris between 1586 and 1600. Its long gallery is the largest Renaissance vaulted hall in Northern Europe and the walls are lined by an impressive collection of classical statuary from the ancient world. The ceilings and window surrounds are covered in 'grotesque' frescoes, so-called because they imitate the ancient Roman frescoes used to decorate Nero's garden in Rome.

Mixed among the fantastical beasts and foliage patterns that typify this style are over 100 views of towns in Bavaria, painted between 1588 and 1596. The Residenz buildings surround several exquisite courtyards. The arcaded Grottenhof (Grotto Court) has a bronze Perseus fountain dating from 1595 at the centre of an Italianate garden laid out in 1596. The Königsbauhof (King's Building Court) has a mid-17th century statue of Neptune. Best of all is the Brunnenhof (Fountain Court), an octagonal courtyard designed by Hans Krumper, which makes an atmospheric setting for open-air concerts in summer. At its centre is an impressive fountain by Hubert Gerhard. This depicts the four main Bavarian rivers, along with the gods of classical mythology, gathered around a statue of Otto von Wittelsbach.

Treasury

The stunning Schatzkammer der Residenz (Residence treasury) is used to display the 'household jewels' of the Wittelsbach family, along with a number of religious treasures from Bavarian churches and monasteries. Among the earliest works is a Romanesque crucifix (made around 1006) that belonged to Queen Gisela – and one of the most recent is the Royal Bavarian crown of 1806. The show stealer, however, is a gorgeous statuette of St George killing the Dragon, a Renaissance masterpiece made for Wilhelm V around 1597.

Cuvilliés Theater

This splendid rococo building resulted from the collaboration of Bavaria's greatest 18th-century artists. The architect, after whom the theatre is named, was François Cuvilliés the Elder – Court Dwarf to Maximilian III Joseph before becoming court architect. The ornately decorated boxes are ranged in tiers either side of the Elector's box and strict protocol was observed – the higher your status, the higher up in the theatre you were allowed to sit. The theatre was completed in 1750 and witnessed the first performance of Mozart's *Idomeneo* in January 1781.

Max-Joseph-Platz 3. Tel: (089) 290 67225; www.schloesserbayern.de. Residenz, Treasury & Cuvilliés Theater open: daily, Apr–15 Oct 9am–6pm, Thur until 8pm; 16 Oct–Mar 10am–4pm. Admission charge. U-Bahn: 3, 4, 5 & 6 to Odeonsplatz; tram: 19 to Nationaltheater; bus: 52.

The vast Antiquarium is decorated with Renaissance frescoes and classical sculpture

Schackgalerie

Count Schack (1815–94) bequeathed the paintings in this fine collection to the city of Munich in the late 19th century, having spent his life as a patron of promising artists and well-established names. Some of the pictures were specially commissioned by Count Schack and others were collected on his travels. The collection survives as a representative memorial of fashionable artistic patronage of the day. Here is a perhaps unrivalled exhibition of German Romantic, Idealist and Post-Romantic work by artists such as Marées, Lensbach, Böcklin and Feuerbach.

Prinzregentenstrasse 9. Tel: (089) 2380 5224; www.schack-galerie.de. Open: Wed–Sun, 10am–5pm. Closed: Mon & Tue. Admission charge. U-Bahn: 4 & 5 to Lehel; tram: 17 to Nationalmuseum; bus: 100.

SiemensForum

The Siemens electronics company was founded by Werner Siemens in 1847 and was based in Berlin until it moved to Munich in 1954. This company-run museum looks at the history of electrotechnology and its infinite applications. There are plenty of hands-on displays, including futuristic computer equipment and pioneering electronics from the 19th century.

Oskar-von-Miller-Ring 20. Tel: (089) 636 32660. Open: Sun–Fri 9am–5pm, every first Tue of the month until 9pm. Closed: Sat. Free admission. U-Bahn: 3 & 6 to Odeonsplatz; bus: 100 to Odeonsplatz.

Spielzeug Museum (Toy Museum)

The tiny entrance to this museum, at the foot of a tower in the Altes Rathaus (Old Town Hall), is marked by a quaint mechanical device that whirrs and clangs every few minutes – a kind of eccentric music box. Spiral steps lead up to rooms crammed with every object half-remembered from childhood. The toys here cover a span of 200 years, ranging from the simplest of wooden dolls to sophisticated doll's houses and model railways. This is a great place to see teddy bears, toy soldiers, model cars and dolls, all enjoying a dignified retirement.

Altes Rathaus, Marienplatz. Tel: (089) 294 001. Open: Mon–Sun 10am–5.30pm. Admission charge. U-Bahn: 3 & 6; S-Bahn, & bus 52 to Marienplatz.

Staatliche Münzsammlung (State Coin Collection)

This is a major collection of its kind, with coins from all over the world dating back to antiquity. It is, nevertheless, of obviously specialised interest.

Residenzstrasse 1. Tel: (089) 227 221. Open: Tue, Wed, Fri–Sun 10am–5pm. Closed: Mon & Thur. Admission charge, except on Sun. U-Bahn: 3, 4, 5 & 6 to Odeonsplatz; S-Bahn: to Marienplatz; tram: 19 to Nationaltheater; bus: 53.

Pinakothek der Moderne (Picture Gallery of Modern Art)

Modern art has found a new home in Munich: the important collections formerly housed in the Neue Sammlung (New Collection) and the State Gallery for Modern Art have been transferred to the Pinakothek der Moderne. This museum of 20th- and 21st-century art brushes shoulders with the Old and New Picture Galleries and is the largest museum of its kind in Germany. With an area of some 15,000sq m (160,000sq ft), ample room is now provided for the huge collection of sculpture, painting, video art and photography from the State Gallery for Modern Art, only a fraction of which could be previously seen at its old location in the Haus der Kunst.

Perhaps even more importantly, masterpieces by such major artists as Klee, Picasso, Munch, Dalí and Magritte can now be viewed in conjunction with outstanding examples of the applied arts (art and crafts, modern industrial design) from the Neue Sammlung. Making the overview of modern and contemporary art in all its forms even more comprehensive are architectural drawings and models, as well as examples of the graphic arts from two other city collections.

Barerstrasse 40. Tel: (089) 238 05284; www.museum-der-moderne.de.
Open: Tue–Sun 10am–5pm, Tue & Thur until 8pm. Closed: Mon. U-Bahn: 2 & 8 to Theresienstrasse.

The Altes Rathaus (Old Town Hall) whose tower contains the Spielzeug (Toy) Museum

Stadtmuseum (City Museum)

Much more than just a museum of local history, the Stadtmuseum consists of several exhibitions housed within the city's former arsenal, each one a self-contained display – in other words, a series of museums within a museum. One of the best displays features a superb set of folk dancer puppets carved by Erasmus Grasser in 1480, and now placed, dramatically lit, near the entrance. On various floors there are museums of photography and brewing, and a supremely enjoyable puppet and fairground museum (look for the range of facial expressions on the puppets); elsewhere you will find ancient try-your-strength machines and a gaping King Kong – which moves! The musical instrument collection features every level of music-making sophistication from African bongo drums to the rare Orchestrion – a bygone mechanical music-making contraption that looks like a cross between a piano and an antique cupboard. Look, too, for the before-and-after photographs of the city, in the local history section, showing the effects of World War II bombing.

St Jakobsplatz 1. Tel: (089) 2332 2370; www.stadtmuseum-online.de. Open: Tue–Sun 10am–6pm. Closed: Mon. Admission charge. U-Bahn: 1, 2, 3 & 6 to Sendlinger Tor; S-Bahn: to Marienplatz.

Stuck Villa

The wealthy 'painter prince', Franz von Stuck, had this villa built in 1898 and opted for a fashionable Jugendstil (Art Nouveau) décor. This, together with the artist's own works, provides the theme for the museum's displays of *fin de siècle* furniture and ornaments.

Prinzregentenstrasse 60. Tel: (089) 455 5510; www.villastuck.de. Open: Wed–Sun 11am–6pm. Closed: Mon & Tue. Admission charge. U-Bahn: 4 to Prinzregentenplatz; tram: 18 or bus 100 to Friedensengel.

Theatinerkirche

Dedicated to St Kajetan, this ochre-coloured church was built as a thanks-offering when Henriette Adelaide, wife of Elector Ferdinand Maria, gave birth in 1662 to Crown Prince Maximilian Emanuel. She came from Savoy, and brought in Italian and Swiss architects who created a building along Italian (chiefly Venetian) lines. Finished in 1688 (its tower was added in 1697), the façade was given a rococo aspect in the 1760s by the Cuvilliés, father and son. In the meantime, 17th-century stucco artists had decorated the high altar (whose painting of the Virgin and saints is by Caspar de Crayer, a pupil of Rubens), while Andreas Faistenberger created a sumptuous pulpit in the late 1680s. Today its dome and twin towers add a Latin flourish to the city's skyline, while the mortal remains of Henriette Adelaide and other members of the Wittelsbach family rest in the crypt.

Odeonsplatz. Open: 9am–5.30pm. U-Bahn: 3, 4, 5 & 6 to Odeonsplatz; bus: 52 to Marienplatz.

Valentin Museum (Karl Valentin Museum)

This museum celebrates the eccentric and humorous character of the silent-screen comedian Karl Valentin, the

German Charlie Chaplin. Valentin was wildly popular in the 1920s when Brecht and Hesse were among his followers. The museum is housed in the southern tower of the massive Isartor (Isar Gate), built in 1314 as part of Munich's earliest defences. The mural above the arches, painted in 1825, depicts the triumph of Ludwig the Bavarian after his defeat of the Habsburgs at the Battle of Ampfing in 1322. On the third floor is a little café furnished in the style fashionable at the turn of the 19th century.

Isartorplatz. Tel: (089) 223 266; www.valentin-museum.de. Open: Mon & Tri–Sat 11am–5.30pm, Sun 10am–5.30pm. Admission charge, but free to those over 99. S-Bahn: to Isartor; trams: 17 & 18.

Völkerkundemuseum (State Ethnological Museum)

This museum displays an absorbing miscellany of ethnic bits and pieces from outside Europe, including some spectacular works of folk art, intriguing everyday objects and fine religious artefacts.

Maximilianstrasse 42. Tel: (089) 210 1360. Open: Tue–Sun 9.30am–5.15pm. U-Bahn: 4 & 5 to Lehel; S-Bahn: to Isartorplatz; trams: 17 & 18 to Isartor.

Tourist office
*Hauptbahnhof, Bahnhofplatz 2; Neues Rathaus, Marienplatz
Tel: (089) 233 0300;
fax: (089) 2333 0233;
www.muenchen-tourist.de*

The Theatinerkirche, burial place of members of the Wittelsbach family

Walk: Munich's old city

This walk embraces some of Munich's most fashionable shopping streets and several of its finest squares and monuments.

Allow 2 hours.

Begin in Karlsplatz in front of the Karlstor.

1 Karlstor

This 14th-century city gate sits amid a gracious, semicircular group of buildings built by Gabriel von Seidl in 1900. The statues on the north arch of the Karlstor were sculpted by Konrad Knoll in 1865.

Enter Neuhauser Strasse through the gate.

2 Neuhauser Strasse and the Frauenkirche

This pedestrianised street is the venue of street theatre and buskers. Just beyond the gateway is the pretty Brunnenbuberl fountain of 1895, depicting a satyr spitting on a naked boy. A little further on the left rises the Bürgersaalkirche (*see p33*). Also on the left is the **Alte Akademie**, built by Friedrich Sustris and Wendel Dietrich in the 16th century as a Jesuit college. In front of it stands the voluptuous Richard Strauss fountain, created in 1962 to commemorate the opera *Salome* by the Munich-born composer. Beyond is the Michaelskirche (*see pp38–9*).

Turn left along curving Augustinerstrasse to reach Frauenplatz and the Frauenkirche, Munich's cathedral (see p37). Afterwards, walk back from the cathedral along Liebfrauenstrasse to Kaufingerstrasse and turn left to reach Marienplatz.

3 Marienplatz and the Viktualienmarkt

Marienplatz, abutted by the Neues

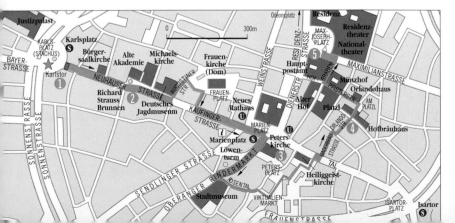

Waiting for the Glockenspiel on Marienplatz

Rathaus (*see p41*), forms the heart of the city. Just beyond the far corner of the square stands **Peterskirche**, Munich's oldest parish church (*see p43*), with a tower affectionately called the Alter Peter (Old Peter).

Continue past Alter Peter to the brick battlemented Löwenturm (Lion Tower), a medieval water tower, and turn left into Rosental, with its bookshops and jewellers. This leads to the Viktualienmarkt, Munich's famous food market (*see p142*).

Turn left in Viktualienmarkt, heading north to the street called Tal, and you will find the **Heiliggeistkirche** (Holy Ghost Church), founded in 1208 but rebuilt by Johann Georg Ettenhofer from 1724. Its finest treasure is the *Madonna* (1450).

4 The way to Max-Joseph-Platz
From the north side of the Heiliggeist-kirche follow Tal; turn first left in Maderbräustrasse, right in Ledererstrasse, then first left into Orlandostrasse. This will bring you to

Am Platzl and the **Orlandohaus**, named after the 16th-century Dutch musician Orlando di Lasso, who was Kapell-meister at the court of Albrecht V. The Hofbräuhaus (the celebrated beer hall – *see p37*) juts out into the same square. From Am Platzl, Pfisterstrasse runs alongside the Münzhof, Bavaria's former mint (*see p39*).
Turn right along Hofgraben, which joins Maximilianstrasse, where you turn left to reach Max-Joseph-Platz.

5 Max-Joseph-Platz
Laid out by Leo von Klenze and Karl von Fischer in the 1830s, Max-Joseph-Platz surrounds a monument to Bavaria's first king, Maximilian I Joseph. Behind the king's back is Bavaria's Nationaltheater, the state opera house (*see p40*). On the south side of the square is the Hauptpostamt (former main post office), a rococo palace transformed in the Italian style by von Klenze in the late 1830s, while on the north side rises the Residenz (*see pp46–7*).

Walk: royal Munich

This relatively easy walk meanders around the short stretch of central Munich distinguished by graceful palaces and elegant squares presided over by beautifully detailed statues.

Allow 2 hours.

Begin at Odeonsplatz.

1 Odeonsplatz

Odeonsplatz centres on an equestrian statue of King Ludwig I and is named after the Odeon (No 3), a concert hall (now offices) designed by Leopold von Klenze in 1826. It is matched by the Leuchtenberg-Palais (No 4), which Klenze built a year later for the Duke of Leuchtenberg. Between them, further back in Wittelsbacherplatz, you can see the palace he built for Prince Ludwig Ferdinand. To the south of Odeonsplatz is the **Feldherrnhalle**, built in the early

1840s. It shelters statues of two Bavarian generals: Tilly (1559–1632), who fought in the Thirty Years' War, and Wrede (1767–1838), hero of the Napoleonic Wars. In the middle arch, the statue of a soldier brandishing his standard is a memorial to the Bavarian army which fought in the Franco-Prussian War of 1870–71. Nearby is the Palais Preysing, built by Josepf Effner between 1723 and 1728. Opposite, on Theatinerstrasse, is the Theatinerkirche (*see p50*).

To the east of Odeonsplatz is the **Hofgarten**. Laid out for Duke Maximilian I between 1613 and 1617 in

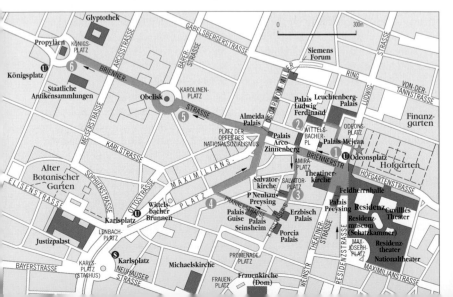

the Italian Renaissance style, the garden has an octagonal temple to Diana, topped by her statue (by Hubert Gerhart, 1594) and four putti by Hans Krumper.
Take Briennerstrasse to reach Wittels-bacherplatz on the right.

2 Wittelsbacherplatz

Wittelsbacherplatz also centres on an equestrian statue, a bronze of Elector Maximilian I. Palais Méjean (1824) shades this square on the elector's left, Klenze's Palais Arco-Zinnenberg (1820) on his right.
Walk along Amiraplatz into Salvatorplatz.

3 Around Salvatorplatz

Here is the Salvatorkirche, a late-Gothic brick church built by Lukas Rottaler in the 1490s. A short way further south, on the left of Kardinal-Faulhaber-Strasse, stands the **Porcia Palais**, built by Enrico Zuccalli, with an exquisite façade designed by Cuvilliés the Elder in 1733; it has a superb rococo façade by Johann Baptist Zimmermann. Note the pretty statue of the Virgin Mary over its portal.
Walk west from here along Prannerstrasse.

4 Prannerstrasse and Maximiliansplatz

You will pass the Palais Neuhaus-Preysing (No 2), another masterpiece by Cuvilliés (1737), the Palais Seinsheim (No 7; built in 1764), and Palais Guise (No 9; built around 1765) before reaching Maximiliansplatz. Pass through a monumental broken archway into the shady square, which is dotted with statues of local worthies. To the left is the celebrated Wittelsbacher Brunnen (Fountain), designed by Adolf von

Hildebrandt and erected in 1895 in honour of the house of Wittelsbach.
Turn right, walking past the statue of Schiller which looks across Briennerstrasse, on the far side of which stands the classical Almeida Palais, built by Métivier in 1824. A short detour north, along Oskar-von-Miller-Ring, takes you to the SiemensForum (see p48).

5 Briennerstrasse

Briennerstrasse now runs west to the Obelisk, which was cast out of Turkish cannons in 1833 and set up in memory of 30,000 Bavarian soldiers, conscripted into Napoleon's army, killed in Russia.
Carry on into Königsplatz.

6 Königsplatz

Laid out in 1815 to the designs of Karl von Fischer on the orders of King Maximilian I, Königsplatz is surrounded by three imposing neoclassical buildings: the Antikensammlungen and the Glyptothek (*see p29*), plus the Propyläen. The latter was designed by Klenze between 1848 and 1862 in Greek Doric style and was modelled on the Acropolis in Athens; it commemorates Greece's fight for freedom against Turkey (the Greek king at that time was the son of Ludwig I of Bavaria).

Cuvilliés' Palais Neuhaus-Preysing

Munich environs

Dachau

Dachau has the misfortune to suffer worldwide notoriety as the site of the Third Reich's first concentration camp, established in a former munitions factory on the edge of this small town, now itself engulfed within Munich's commuter-belt hinterlands.

KZ Gedenkstätte (Concentration Camp Memorial)

Today the camp is preserved as a memorial to the 206,000 people who died there, with the bleak facts about human experiments, disease, punishment and torture presented soberingly in a display housed within the former administration block. Interestingly, only a small percentage of these were Jews; this camp held members of the Reichstag and other political prisoners as well as Catholic priests and bishops. An informative but disturbing 30-minute film is shown throughout the day (in English at 11.30am and 3.30pm). The crematorium, whose ovens were kept going day and night, and the gas chambers (never used) have been preserved. Much of the camp has been flattened, but a reconstructed block gives an idea of the bleak living conditions the prisoners had to endure. A replica of the original gate bears the bitterly ironic legend *Arbeit macht Frei* ('Work makes Freedom'), while the multilingual memorial announces 'Never again'. Here, too, are a memorial to the Jews, a Protestant church of reconciliation and a Catholic chapel.

Dachau Town

The old town, perched above the river Amper, retains enough charm in its winding cobblestone streets to merit a walkabout from the station. St Jakob's Church (1584–1629) is a prominent landmark, though uninteresting from within, close to the Schloss (castle), with its monumental staircase and coffered ceiling. The Hofgarten terrace garden offers fine views down upon Munich. Around the turn of the 20th century, Dachau was home to a bustling artist colony – many were attracted to paint here because of the natural lighting effects found in the heathy Dachauer Moos; the Gemälderie gallery displays works by the group, while the Bezirksmuseum of local history has rustic bygones and more. *Concentration camp open: Tue–Sun 9am–5pm. Closed: Mon. Free admission. Gemälderie & Bezirksmuseum open: Wed–Fri 11am–5pm, Sat & Sun 1–5pm. S-Bahn: S2 (direction Petershausen) to Dachau, then bus 724 or 726 from station to KZ Gedenkstätte.*

Ramersdorf

One of Bavaria's oldest pilgrimage churches is St Maria in Ramersdorf, generally known as the Ramersdorf-kircherl. Although a church has existed here since the 11th century, the present magical building dates from 1399 and was given its baroque décor in 1675. The belfry is surmounted by a baroque onion dome. The rich interior, whose ceiling motifs are picked out in gold, converges on the baroque high altar, on which sits a miracle-working

Madonna and Child sculpted by Erasmus Grasser around 1480. He contributed another masterpiece to this church: a *Crucifixion* altarpiece (1483) carved with expressive figures beneath the Cross and four side panels depicting Christ's Passion. The back of the altarpiece is further enriched with paintings by Jan Polack. Another painting of 1635 shows 32 hostages taken from Munich in the Thirty Years' War.

The nuns will unlock the side door for access to the body of the church; otherwise you can see nearly everything from the west end through a large metal grille. On Saturday mornings a small flea market sets up opposite the church. *U-Bahn: 1 to Karl-Preis-Platz; bus: 95 to Ramersdorf. From U-Bahn station walk south along Rosenheimer Strasse, then turn left into Aribonenstrasse.*

Schloss Blutenburg

Duke Albrecht III built this small moated hunting lodge on the site of a former fortress. His son, Duke Sigismund, completed the island castle in 1488 by adding a chapel, built in the late Gothic style by the same architects that designed Munich cathedral. The chapel has three outstanding altarpieces by Jan Polack, dating from 1488–95. Also displayed here is the *Blutenberg Madonna*, from the workshops of Erasmus Grasser. *Open: daily, summer 9am–5pm; winter 10am–4pm. S-Bahn: to Pasing, then bus 73, 75 or 76 to Blutenburg.*

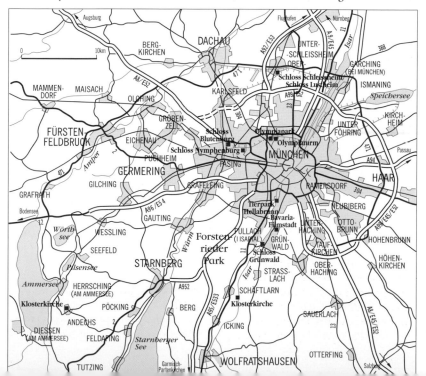

Schloss Grünwald

Schloss (or Burg) Grünwald, 13km
(8 miles) south of Munich, began life
as a 13th-century Gothic fortress; some
parts, including the tower, remain
picturesquely medieval. In the 1480s,
after it fell into the possession of the
Wittelsbachs, the castle was enlarged by
the addition of a magnificent porch,
decorated with coats of arms. Later the
castle served as a prison and then as an
armoury. Now it is a museum displaying
prehistoric and Roman antiquities.
*Zellerstrasse 3, Grünwald. Tel: (089) 641
3218. Open: 15 Mar–30 Nov, Wed–Sun
10am–4.30pm. Closed: Mon & Tue.
Admission charge. S-Bahn: 7 to
Höllriegelskreuth; tram: 25 to Grünwald.*

Schloss Nymphenburg
The Schloss

The approach to Schloss Nymphenburg,
along its swan-populated canal (a
popular midwinter haunt of skaters and
ice-hockey enthusiasts), at once presents
a picture of striking symmetry – belying
the fact that the palace was built over a
century by four members of the
Wittelsbach family. Although built as a
summer country residence, it is now
well engulfed by the western suburbs.

Several leading architects of the late
17th and 18th centuries contributed
their mastery to this palace and its
surrounding buildings. Agostino Barelli
designed the central pavilion between
1664 and 1674, a gift from the Elector
Ferdinand Maria to his wife Henriette
Adelaide. Antonio Viscardi extended it
in 1702 on behalf of Elector Maximilian
Emanuel, adding side pavilions
connected to the main house by

galleries. Then, in 1715, Joseph Effner
added the wings, replacing the Italianate
style of the previous architects with one
based on French models. The interior
displays some sumptuous baroque
decoration, including a splendidly
frescoed great hall. Here, too, is King
Ludwig I's celebrated 'Gallery of
Beauties', 36 portraits of the king's
favourites, including his mistresses Lola
Montez and Helene Sedlmayr; these
were painted by Josef Stieler between
1827 and 1850.

The park

In many ways it is the park, with its
hunting lodges, temples and pavilions,
that is the most attractive feature of
Nymphenburg. The park covers
221 hectares (546 acres) and was
redesigned by the brilliant landscape
gardener Friedrich Ludwig von Sckell in
1805. Here Effner built the baroque
pleasure house called the Pagodenburg
(1719) which stands beside the
smaller of the two lakes in the
palace grounds.

Effner followed this with the
Badenburg, a bathing lodge at the
corner of the great lake, finished in
1721. Each has a baroque parterre with
waterworks. Then came his
Magdalenenklause, a bizarre shell-
encrusted mock-ruin designed as a
hermitage, completed in 1728 and
furnished with a grotto chapel and a
statue of St Mary Magdalen.

As a present for his wife Amalia,
Maximilian Emanuel's son, Karl
Albrecht, commissioned Cuvilliés the
Elder to design the sumptuous, rococo
Amalienburg (1734). This was decorated

with stucco work and frescoes by Johann Baptist Zimmermann and his brothers, and has a swirlingly decorated hall of mirrors: if you stand in the centre of the hall, you will see yourself reflected tenfold.

The Marstallmuseum
(Royal Stables Museum)

This absorbing museum exhibits the products of the Nymphenburg porcelain factory, founded here in 1747, and has royal sleighs and carriages: one can imagine the Wittelsbachs riding them through this great estate.

Schloss Nymphenburg, Eingang 1. Tel: (089) 179 080; www.schloesser.bayern.de. Schloss and Marstallmuseum open: 1 Apr–15 Oct daily 9am–6pm, winter 10am–4pm. (For park see pp133–4.) U-Bahn: 1 to Rotkreuzplatz, then tram 12 to Romanplatz; tram: 17 & bus 51 to Schloss Nymphenburg.

Schloss Nymphenburg, though built over a hundred years, is exceptionally harmonious

Schloss Schleissheim and Schloss Lustheim

The long white façade of Schloss Schleissheim was built on a scale to rival Versailles, and is reflected in a wide, round artificial pond. Maximilian Emanuel, the Great Elector, commissioned the building in 1701 from the Italian architect Zuccalli. During the War of the Spanish Succession, the Elector was defeated at the battle of Höchstädt and fled to France, so that work on his Schloss ceased from 1704 to 1719. The building was finally completed by the Bavarian architect Joseph Effner in 1725.

Other celebrated masters added to its glory, particularly Ignaz Günther who created the east portal in 1763, and Johann Baptist Zimmermann, who stuccoed the Festival Hall and the magnificent staircase. The former has a ceiling fresco by the Italian Jacopo Amigoni depicting the exploits of Aeneas. The staircase ceiling was frescoed by Cosmas Damien Asam, who also decorated the Elector's chapel with scenes from the life of St Maximilian.

The Schloss makes an ideal setting for the baroque works of art on show; these include paintings from other countries, particularly Italian masterpieces, from the Bavarian National Museum's extensive collections.

Schloss Schleissheim is known as the Neues (New) Schloss to distinguish it from the Renaissance Altes (Old) Schloss, which had been built in the early 17th century for Duke Maximilian I by the architect Heinrich Schön and decorated by Peter Candid. Today, it serves, amongst other things, as a gallery devoted to the Christian year and to religious folk art from all over the world.

At the far side of the splendid formal park surrounding Schloss Schleissheim is another fine palace, Schloss Lustheim. This was built in the Italian baroque style by Enrico

The graceful symmetry of Schloss Schleissheim, built to rival Versailles

Elephants at the Tierpark Hellabrunn

Zuccalli in 1684 on the occasion of the marriage of Maximilian Emanuel of Bavaria to Maria Antonia, daughter of the Emperor Leopold I.

This exquisite building has a festival hall with a mirrored vault and frescoes depicting *Diana the Huntress* by Francesco Rosa, Johann Trubillio and Johann Gumpp. A huge oil painting depicts scenes from the life of Maximilian Emanuel.

The philanthropist Ernst Schneider donated his collection of Meissen porcelain to the state in 1968, on the condition that it be exhibited in a baroque palace. This splendid legacy of nearly 2,000 pieces dating from 1710 to 1800 is displayed here in 15 rooms. *Neues Schloss, Altes Schloss & Schloss Lustheim. Tel: (089) 315 8720. Open: Tue–Sun 9am–6pm (until 4pm from Oct–Mar). Closed: Mon. S-Bahn: 1 to Oberschleissheim; bus: 292. Admission charge.*

Tierpark Hellabrunn (Hellabrunn Zoo)

The zoo abuts the banks of the Isar and is located southwest of the city centre. It has over 8,000 animals, roaming in open enclosures in a semi-natural habitat. There is also a walk-in aviary. *Tierparkstrasse 30. Tel: (089) 625 080; www.zoo-munich.de. Open: daily, Apr–Sept 8am–6pm; Oct–Mar 9am–5pm. Admission charge. U-Bahn: 3 to Thalkirchen; bus: 52 to end of route.*

Near Hellabrunn, Flauchersteg is a popular place for swimming in the River Isar or enjoying picnics and barbecues on the stony beach. Summer weekends are crowded.

Southeast Bavaria

Bad Reichenhall

The Celts were probably the first to exploit the underground springs of this spa, where both the saline water and the salt derived from it are considered to have significant curative powers. Today, the town also produces salt from the springs and underground lakes of nearby Berchtesgaden, whose waters are pumped here through pipes stretching for 18km (11 miles).

Alte Saline

These former salt works were built at the

beginning of the 16th century and then greatly enlarged under Ludwig I in 1834. The 19th-century artist Moritz von Schwind painted the series of frescoes that decorate the factory chapel. The guided tour takes in several exhibitions detailing the history of salt mining from ancient times to the present day.
Salinenstrasse. Tel: (0 8651) 700 2146;

www.alte-saline-bad-reichenhall.de. Open: May–Oct, daily 10am–4pm; Nov–Apr, Tue–Fri & the first Sun of the month from 2–4pm. Admission charge.

St Ägidien

This Carmelite church was begun in 1159 in the Romanesque style but was then Gothicised, in part, in the 15th century. Today, its most important feature is a series of modern wall paintings depicting several harrowing events that took place in Bad Reichenhall during World War II.

One of these portrays an Allied bombing raid of 1945 that killed 224 citizens; the four horsemen of the Apocalypse can be seen riding above the conflagration. Another shows the church's anti-Nazi parish priest who vanished in Dachau.
Poststrasse. Open: 9am–5.30pm.

St Zeno

This is the largest Romanesque basilica in Upper Bavaria. Founded in 1208, it suffered fire damage in the Middle Ages and, as a result, parts of the church were rebuilt in the Gothic style. In the Romanesque cloister, there is a chapel inscribed FRIDERICUS IMP in thanks for the generosity of Holy Roman Emperor Frederick Barbarossa (1123–90).
Salzburgerstrasse 32. Open: 9am–5.30pm.

Bad Reichenhall is in the extreme southeast of Bavaria, 135km (84 miles) from Munich.
Tourist office: Wittelsbacherstrasse 15. Tel: (08651) 6060; fax: (08651) 606 133; www.bad-reichenhall.de

Bad Tölz

The spa town of Bad Tölz stands on the River Isar at the foot of the Bavarian Alps and it has a noted boys' choir. Just 3km (2 miles) west of the town, the Blombergbahn chairlift carries visitors up Mount Blomberg for mountain walks in the summer and to the ski runs in winter.

Christmas in Bad Tölz

Just outside the town, on the road northeast to Holzkirchen, a signpost directs you off the Bundestrasse 13 road to Sachsenkam and Kloster Reutberg. Here you will find a monastic church built in the early 1730s, whose Madonna and Child came from Loreto in Italy. There is also a former monastic brewery whose beer can still be sampled at the nearby Bräustüberl (Beer Hall).

Franziskanerkirche

Built in the 1730s for Franciscan monks, the baroque church rises above the Isar in the War Memorial Gardens.
For information about opening hours, tel: (08041) 76960, or inquire at the tourist office.

Maria Himmelfahrt

This church, dedicated to the Virgin Mary in her Assumption, was rebuilt in the late Gothic style after a fire in 1453 destroyed the older church. Superb stained glass, made around 1500, depicts the Nativity. The apse tracery is magical, as is a baroque Madonna on the arch of the choir, carved by Bartholomäus Steinle in 1611. The entrance to the 16th-century Winzerer chapel is frescoed with portraits of St Sebastian and St Roch, both of whom are reputed to be able to protect the faithful against plague.
Open: 9am–5.30pm. A guided tour is offered as a part of the guided town walk. Inquire at the tourist office.

Marktstrasse

Reached at the top of the town through a gateway dated 1353, the spa's traffic-free main street passes between ancient houses with rich façades and overhanging roofs. A World War I memorial is decorated with reliefs depicting the exploits of the town's 16th-century hero, Kaspar von Winzerer, who takes King François I of France prisoner, jousts with Emperor Maximilian I, and is finally slain in a tournament of 1552. A fourth panel shows Napoleon III of France in flight from Sedan in 1870.

Bad Tölz is 40km (25 miles) south of Munich.

Tourist office: Max Höfler-Platz 1. Tel: (08041) 78670; fax: (08041) 786 756; www.bad-toelz.de (in German only).

The Bavarians share with many Europeans a passion for health cures, and spas have flourished here since the 19th century. Spa towns are usually prefixed by the name Bad (Bath). Most developed around a warm sulphurous or mineral spring with a reputation for its healing properties. Supplementing the curative effects of the water you will find restful parks, along with sporting, recreational and cultural facilities. Bad Griesbach, a spa in the Rottal valley near Passau, is also the national centre of the German golf association.

Among the finest spas in Bavaria are Bad Aibling, west of the town of Rosenheim, and Bad Mergentheim (*see pp110–11*), which prospered after the discovery of a magnesium sulphate spring in 1826, whose waters are said to cure kidney, liver and gall-bladder conditions. Bad Kissingen, in Franconia, was renowned for its curative waters in antiquity and became famous when the waters of its Rakoczy spring, discovered in 1737, attracted European royalty, leading to the building of a casino and four concert halls. Bad Reichenhall (*see p62*) is a spa with saline springs that have been used since pre-Roman times, and at Bad Tölz the therapy is based on peat baths and an iodine spring discovered in 1846.

The therapeutic value of mud baths is also appreciated in Bavaria, a facility offered by many of its spas, for instance in the Ludwigsbad at Murnau, northeast of Oberammergau.

In Munich, along with state-of-the-art day spas, locals love the swimming pools, hot and cold baths, sunbeds, steam bath and other facilities at the beautifully restored Art Nouveau Mullersches Volksbad. *Rosenheimerstr 1. Tel: (089) 2361 3434.*

The beautiful Art Nouveau Mullersches Volksbad

Berchtesgaden

Unjustly remembered as the place where Adolf Hitler had his mountain retreat (although, in fact, the Führer and his Nazi cronies seldom visited the Eagle's Nest Kehlsteinhaus – *see page 75*), Berchtesgaden is, in fact, a medieval town surrounded by nine Alpine peaks, of which the 2,713-m (8,901-ft) high Watzmann is the second highest in Germany.

Königliches Schloss Berchtesgaden

A former monastery, Berchtesgaden's castle then became the principal seat of the town's rulers before finally passing into the hands of the Wittelsbach family in 1810. Guided tours begin with the Romanesque cloister and take you through rooms containing statues by Tilman Riemenschneider and Erasmus Grasser, paintings by Cranach the Elder and memorabilia of the Wittelsbach dynasty.
Marktplatz. Tel: (08652) 947 980.
Open: Whitsuntide–15 Oct, Sun–Fri 10am–noon & 2–4pm (closed Sat); 16 Oct–Whitsuntide, Mon–Fri 11am–2pm (closed weekends).
Guided tours only. Admission charge.

Marktplatz

The triangular market square of Berchtesgaden is flanked by painted Renaissance and baroque houses and centres on an 1860s fountain.

St Maria am Anger

This church was built between 1488 and 1519 (tower 1682) and contains some superb sculptures. It stands next to a graveyard where the first tomb on the right is that of Anton Adler, who died in 1822 at the great age of 117.
On-Imhof-Strasse. Open: 9am–5.30pm.

Stiftskirche St Peter und St Johannes

The former church of St Peter and St John has symmetrical 13th-century towers (with 19th-century spires). Through its 12th-century Romanesque entrance, you reach a nave built around 1200 and a choir added 100 years later, the whole topped by lovely Gothic vaulting. Look out for a sculpted Romanesque holy water stoup, and the red marble tombs of the provosts who ruled Berchtesgaden until the Wittelsbach family took over.

Berchtesgaden is 147km (91 miles) southeast of Munich.
Tourist office: Königsseer Strasse 2.
Tel: (08652) 9670; fax: (08652) 967 400;
www.berchtesgaden.com

Chiemsee

With a surface area of 82sq km (32sq miles), Chiemsee is the largest lake in Bavaria. Its banks are sheltered by wooded hills and rich pastures. Of the islands dotting the lake, the **Herreninsel** (Men's Island) is the largest.

Underground mines

A visit to the underground salt mines at Bergwerkallee, Berchtesgaden, is enthralling. The miners act as guides, helping you to dress in miners' protective clothing, slide down a chute, travel on a little train and float across an underground lake.
Guided tours: May–mid-Oct, daily 9am–5pm; otherwise Mon–Sat 12.30–3.30pm.
Tel: (08652) 60020. Admission charge.

Here a Benedictine monastery was founded in the 8th century and flourished until 1803, though all that remains today is the Gothic church and the 'old palace' with its imperial hall. On the same island is Schloss Herrenchiemsee, the unfinished replica of the Château of Versailles built for King Ludwig II (*see pp94–5*). The buildings include the fabulous Hall of Mirrors, a monumental staircase, a huge circular bathroom and the gilded royal bedchamber (*guided tours only: Apr–3 Oct 9am–6pm, 4–31 Oct 9.40am–5pm, rest of the year 9.40am–4pm. Admission charge*).

The **Fraueninsel** (Women's Island) is so-called after the Benedictine nunnery, founded in the 8th century, whose nuns still distil and sell a liqueur of their own. Their chapel, rebuilt in the 12th century, has an 8th-century door knocker. Inside are 11 baroque altars. North of this chapel rises the Torhalle, a stone gatehouse built around 860, whose upper storey is decorated with modern reproductions of medieval frescoes (*open: Whitsuntide–Sept 11am–6pm*).

The fishermen of the Fraueninsel fish the lake in the morning; their families smoke the catch in the afternoon and then sell it from their homes, wrapped in paper napkins, and ready to eat.

Of the towns surrounding the lake the loveliest is **Prien am Chiemsee**, whose baroque church of Maria Himmelfahrt (decorated by Johann Baptist Zimmermann) has a separate Gothic, onion-domed baptistry (*open: 9am–5.30pm*). From the railway station, a late 19th-century steam train runs along a single-line track carrying visitors

Snowy peaks rise in the crystal-clear air of Alpine Berchtesgaden

to the harbour. From here you can have a choice of several different boat trips that will take you to one or both of the main islands, or to the other attractive towns that are set beside the lake. A timetable of sailings can be downloaded from *www.chiemsee-schifffahrt.de*

Chiemsee lies 90km (56 miles) east of Munich. Tourist office: Alte Rathausstrasse 11, Prien am Chiemsee. Tel: (08051) 69050; fax: (08051) 690 540; www.prien.chiemsee.de

Erding

The 17th-century feel of this little town derives from the fact that many of its buildings were gutted in a fire of 1648. Only one medieval gateway, built around 1500, with a later onion dome, remains, as do a few remnants of the 14th-century defensive wall. The Heiliggeistspital, a hospice founded in 1444, stands to the south of this gateway, alongside its medieval chapel (with a high altar of 1793). One of the first buildings to be restored after the fire was the Rathaus, the little town hall in Landshuterstrasse that was formerly home to the Counts of Preysing. St Johannes, the town's parish church, is a magnificent 14th- and 15th-century Gothic basilica built of brick.
30km (19 miles) northeast of Munich. Tourist office: Landshuterstrasse 1 or 12. Tel: (08122) 558 488; fax: (08122) 558 489; www.erding-tourist.de

Freising

Freising was formerly the seat of the archbishop who is now based in Munich, hence the superb cathedral. Benedictine monks set up one of the world's oldest breweries, Weihenstephan (*www.brauerei-weihenstephan.de*), here in the 11th century. Set on a hill above the River Isar, the cathedral (Dom) was begun in the mid-12th century and was richly decorated by the Asam brothers in the 1720s. Its high altar is a Renaissance gem, dating from 1625. In the Romanesque crypt lie the bones of the 8th-century missionary St Korbinian, to whom (along with the Virgin Mary) the cathedral is dedicated. It rises in a close filled with exquisite old buildings.

The Diocesan Museum has sculptures by Erasmus Grasser and Hans Leinberger, paintings by Jan Polack and a gallery of baroque paintings.
Cathedral open: 9am–5.30pm.
Diocesan Museum open: Tue–Sun 10am–5pm. Closed: Mon.
Freising is 30km (19 miles) north of Munich.
Tourist office: Marienplatz 7.
Tel: (08161) 54122; fax: (08161) 54231; www.freising.de (in German only).

Landshut

Dominated by Traunitz Castle, which sits on a ridge above the town, this former capital of Lower Bavaria lies on the banks of the River Isar surrounded by forested hills. At the heart of the modern city is the old city, a medieval and Renaissance pearl, whose two main streets, the Altstadt and the Neustadt, run parallel to each other, connected by narrow alleys.

Altstadt is lined by fine step-gabled 15th- and 16th-century houses and several arcaded courtyards. One of its principal buildings is the Rathaus, the three-gabled town hall formed from three medieval houses. The 19th-century frescoes inside illustrate the lavish wedding that took place in Landshut between Duke George and a Polish princess in 1475, a wedding that is restaged in the town every third year as part of a festive pageant. Rising opposite the town hall is the Residenz, built for Duke Ludwig X in the 1530s and 1540s. Ludwig's admiration for the Italian Renaissance is mirrored in the 40 rooms of this palace, which has now become the perfect setting for an art gallery (the Staatsgalerie art gallery in the

Residenz keeps the same hours as Burg Trausnitz, except that it is closed on Monday – *see below*).

The gently curving Altstadt is closed off at one end by the Gothic church of St Martin, designed by Hans Stethaimer, and built out of rose-pink brick between 1389 and 1500. Its spire, at 133m (436ft), is the tallest built of brick in the world. Five flamboyant Gothic porches pierce its walls, which are clad with memorial tablets (including a bust of

Stethaimer himself and his coat of arms bearing two set squares). The lavish Gothic altar was carved in 1424, its baroque upper half dating from 1664. In front of the chancel hangs a crucifix carved by Michael Erhart in 1495. The choir stalls, of around 1500, carry beautiful carvings of biblical scenes.

Above the town is Burg (Castle) Trausnitz, founded in 1204. It was later enriched by Prince William of

Beautifully maintained buildings in Freising

Bavaria with a Renaissance-style gallery courtyard and a famous staircase (the Narrentreppe) frescoed in 1578 with figures from the Italian Commedia dell'Arte. As one might well expect, there are splendid views over the town from the castle walls (*guided tours from Apr–Sept 9am–6pm; Oct–Mar open 10am–4pm; admission charge*).
65km (40 miles) northeast of Munich. *Tourist office: in the Rathaus (Town Hall), Veldener Strasse 15. Tel: (0871) 408 128; fax: (0871) 408 16128; www.landkreis-landshut.de*

Passau

Three rivers, the Danube, the Inn and the Ilz, all meet at Passau, which was settled by the Celts in pre-Christian times. Converted to Christianity in the mid-5th century, it was elevated to the bishopric status by St Boniface in 739. To see Passau from its most beautiful vantage points, and to fully appreciate its setting, view it from the fortress high on

Passau's enormous cathedral rises serenely above the River Inn

the opposite side of the river and from the river itself on a 'Three Rivers Tour' (*offered every 30 minutes, 10am–5pm in summer and hourly 11am–3pm the rest of the year*). *Mooring 7/8, opposite the Rathaus. Tel: (0851) 929 292; www.donauschifffahrt.de*

Alte Residenz and Neue Residenz

Both palaces sit in Residenzplatz, the first built for the bishops in Renaissance style, the second in baroque. In the same square is a 13th-century pharmacy. The Neue Residenz exhibits the cathedral treasury and is the diocesan museum. *Open: May–Oct 10am–4pm. Closed: Sun.*

Glass Museum

The size and complexity of the glass collections housed adjacent to the Hotel Wilder Mann are truly mind-boggling. These concentrate especially on European and Bohemian glass from 1650 to 1950, and the Art Nouveau era is especially well covered. *Rathausplatz. Tel: (0851) 35071;*

www.wilder-mann.com. Open: daily 1–5pm. Admission charge.

Stephansdom

Passau's cathedral has an octagonal dome that dominates the city. Founded in the 5th century and rebuilt from 1407, it was comprehensively rebuilt again after a fire in 1680 by Carlo Lurago. Its organ, the largest church organ in the world (built in 1928 with over 17,754 pipes and 238 stops), is played Monday to Saturday at noon and and also at 7.30pm on Thursdays from May to October. Below, the cathedral square is surrounded by lovely canons' houses. *Open: 9am–5.30pm.*

Veste Niederhaus and Veste Oberhaus

These citadels were built respectively in the early 13th and 14th centuries to consolidate the hold of the bishops on the city. Veste Oberhaus houses the city and regional museums. *Tel: (0851) 493 350; www.oberhausmuseum.de. Open: 8 Apr– 5 Nov, Mon–Fri 9am–5pm, weekends & holidays 10am–6pm.*

Passau is 150km (93 miles) northeast of Munich. Tourist office: Rathausplatz 3. Tel: (0851) 955 980; fax: (0851) 35107; www.tourismuspassau.de

Wasserburg Am Inn

This walled town sits on the River Inn opposite a 15th-century castle. You enter by a river bridge and through a battlemented medieval gateway, built in 1374, and decorated in 1568 with a pair of hairy-faced knights. The fortified gateway across the bridge, called Brucktor, abuts on to Wasserburg's former Holy Ghost hospice (founded in 1341). Forming part of the building complex is a church with an impressive 16th-century altar, and an art gallery (Erstes Imaginäres Museum) displaying reproductions of works ranging from Romanesque frescoes to the paintings of Picasso (*open: May–Sept 11am–5pm; Oct–Apr 1–5pm; closed: Mon*).

The charming Marienplatz includes Wasserburg's 65-m (213-ft) high medieval watchtower, saved from a fire in 1874 by the intervention of the Virgin Mary, according to local belief. Opposite is the town's former tollhouse (the Altes Mauthaus), which was built for the Duke of Bavaria in 1497 and given a Renaissance façade with oriel windows in 1530. In the same square is the late Gothic Rathaus (town hall) built in the mid-15th century by Jörg Tünzl (*guided tours on the hour, except Mondays*). Opposite is the Kernhaus with a stucco façade of 1738 by Johann Baptist Zimmermann.

The church of St Jakob was begun in 1410 and completed in 1461. Inside, little has changed since then, save for the addition of a rich Renaissance pulpit of 1639, by Martin and Michael Zürn.

Wasserburg is 55km (34 miles) east of Munich. Tourist office: in the Rathaus on Marienplatz. Tel: (08071) 10522; fax: (08071) 10521; www.wasserburg.de

---

Mariahilf
On the far side of the River Inn is the baroque pilgrimage church of Mariahilf. Reached by 264 steps, it was built by Francesco Garbiano to enshrine a miracle-working statue of the *Madonna and Child*.

Tour: around Altötting

This circular tour of some 60km (37 miles) visits the Öttinger Forest and captivating towns and villages, passing by nature reserves and along the banks of two rivers. An easy route to follow, it makes an excellent cycle tour, its gradients well within the capacity of children.

Allow 4 hours by car, 8 hours by bicycle.

1 Altötting
Pilgrims have been coming here to seek help from the miracle-working statue of the Black Madonna for several centuries. The statue is in the Gnadenkapelle (Chapel of Grace) on the main square, Kapellplatz. Do not miss the Collegiate Church of St Philip and St Jakob.
Leave Altötting by way of the Alte Poststrasse, travelling southeast through the forest to Emmerting and Hohenwart.

2 Hohenwart
This suburb, across the River Alz from Emmerting, has a little Gothic church dedicated to St Nikolaus, built around 1470.
Continue on to the old town of Burghausen on the River Salzach, which forms the border between Bavaria and Austria.

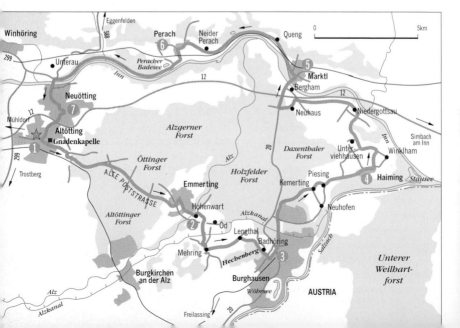

3 Burghausen

The construction of the massive fortress, Germany's largest, was completed in 1253. Part of the building is used to display pictures from the Bavarian state art collection, while elsewhere in the complex you will find a local history museum and a museum of photography.

Continue northeastwards to Haiming.

4 Haiming

Located alongside the Stausee, Haiming has a bird reserve, a castle and the 15th-century church of St Oswald.

Continue north to follow the bank of the River Inn to Niedergottsau (with its 15th-century pilgrimage church), then cross the river to Marktl.

5 Marktl

Set beside the River Inn, Marktl has a lakeside bathing beach, a nature reserve, a local history museum and a

neo-Gothic parish church.

Continue west along the river to Perach.

6 Perach

Here is another attractive lake, for swimming, sailing or sunbathing. The town's Romanesque parish church, Maria Himmelfahrt, was Gothicised in the 15th century.

Continue west along the Inn to Neuötting.

7 Neuötting

The long Marktplatz is closed at each end by a medieval gate and flanked by arcaded houses. Hans Stethaimer designed the superb brick parish church with its 78-m (256-ft) high spire. Begun in 1410, the fine ogival vaulting was completed in the 1620s. The church houses a rococo statue of St Nikolaus carrying three golden balls, a sign that he is the patron saint of pawnbrokers.

Take the road south for 3km (2 miles) to return to Altötting.

Altötting, home of the famous miracle-working Black Madonna

Tour: the Rossfeld-Ringstrasse

The Rossfeld ring road is a superb piece of 1930s' mountain engineering on which you can drive from Oberau to Obersalzberg (or, if you prefer, the other way round). The Ringstrasse is 16.5km (10 1/4 miles) long, has sharp bends and steep gradients. Often used for motor rallies and even displays of vintage cars, it reaches a height of 1,600m (5,249ft).

Allow 1 hour.

From Berchtesgaden, follow the signs indicating Rossfeld and Rossfeldstrasse. Motorists must pay a toll to use the road.

The Ringstrasse passes through a region frequented by skiers and sunbathers alike. Even in winter, when thick snow

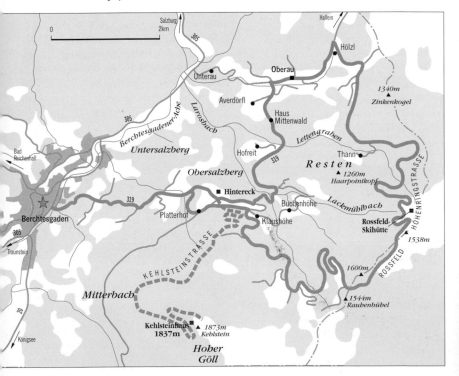

covers the Alps through which the road passes, visitors can be seen seated in deckchairs facing the sun. Along the road there are numerous parking spaces. From these you can often see hang-gliders floating by, virtually at eye level. Snow-clad crags and deep clefts in the rocks appear as you drive. Eventually you will be able to see Bavaria on one side, Austria on the other. You will also see several awesome Alpine peaks. The closest to the Ringstrasse is the Hoher Göll, whose peak reaches 2,522m (8,274ft). Further away, to the southwest, you can see the Watzmann (2,713m/8,901ft). To the east, across the Austrian border, are two mountain ranges – the Tennengebirge and, in the distance, the Dachstein-gebirge whose highest point is 2,996m (9,829ft) above sea level.

Continue to Hintereck, which is the starting point for a visit to the Kehlstein, the once notorious Eagle's Nest. Private cars are no longer allowed along the road from Hintereck to Kehlstein. From the end of May to October access is via a regular bus service that picks up visitors at Hintereck. The last buses leave about 4.25pm. It is also possible to walk to Kehlstein along a 6.5-km (4-mile) long footpath.

Martin Bormann, the Nazi politician, conceived the idea of presenting Adolf Hitler with the Kehlsteinhaus, perched 1,837m (6,027ft) high on a spur of the Hoher Göll above Obersalzberg, on his 50th birthday. Within 13 months a road had been blasted from Obersalzberg up to Kehlstein. The plan was to entertain foreign leaders and diplomats here, but to Bormann's chagrin Hitler never liked the spot and rarely came. Instead, he preferred to entertain such guests as British Prime Minister Neville Chamberlain and French statesman and collaborator Pierre Laval at the chalet in Obersalzberg that he had been renting since 1925.

Although the Allies wished to destroy the Kehlsteinhaus after World War II, the Bürgermeister of Berchtesgaden persuaded them to change their minds. The Eagle's Nest thus became a restaurant from which there are superb views. Its walls, a metre thick, reveal the anxieties of the Hitler régime, and its architecture is a historical monument of that era. Traces also remain of the network of underground shelters that were designed to protect the Nazi leaders (access to these can be gained from the Hotel Türken near the car park in Obersalzberg).

Formidable cliffs and snow-clad crags contrast with mountain meadows

Tour: the Königssee

The green waters of the Königssee, the Bavarians claim, are the cleanest in Germany, and since 1978 the lake and its surroundings have been designated as the Berchtesgaden National Park. Stretching for 8km (5 miles), and 2km (1¼ miles) at its widest, the Königssee is over 190m (623ft) deep and the surrounding cliffs fall almost sheer to the bottom of the lake. Königssee is also surrounded by breathtakingly beautiful mountains, the highest of which is the Watzmann. Throughout the seasons its shores present an ever-changing range of colours, with thick snow in winter, startlingly powerful waterfalls in spring, green vegetation in summer, and finally the rich hues of autumn. *Allow 1¼ hours for the ferry trip.*

To reach the lake you can take a bus from Berchtesgaden's railway station to the village of Königssee. From there, 21 electrically powered boats take passengers across the lake to St Bartholomä.

The clear waters of Königssee

The ferry journey

At various points, the lakeside cliffs give off a resounding echo; the crew may well stop the boat while one of their number blows a trumpet fanfare – everyone waits in silence until the notes are tossed back by the cliffs (the crew will then take a collection). The journey then continues to a small cluster of buildings halfway down the western shore of the lake that is dominated by the baroque church of St Bartholomä.

St Bartholomä

One tower of the church is onion-domed, while the second has a round cap with a jaunty peak. The roof also has three little domes. The church dates back to 1134 and it was a favourite pilgrimage spot for Bavarians (pilgrims still come on 24 August). The priors who once ruled Berchtesgaden had a

Boathouses, inns and balconied chalets cluster round Königssee's shores

hunting lodge here, which is now a restaurant serving fish caught in the lake. When the Berchtesgaden region became Bavarian in 1810 (previously it had been part of Austria) this became a favourite spot of the royal family who made merry hunting and fishing. Shades of the long-dead great haunt this exquisite spot. Here, for example, the royal architect Karl Friedrich Schinkel and the Romantic artist Caspar David Friedrich found rest and inspiration.

Excursion to the Watzmann

Intrepid walkers can join an organised party for the one-hour trek to the east face of the mighty Watzmann.
You can break your journey at St Bartholomä before resuming your ferry journey. A further half-hour sail from St Bartholomä will bring you to Salet. From here a 15-minute walk on a clearly signposted track brings you to the Obersee.

Obersee

The waters of this smaller and wilder-looking lake reflect the Hagen mountain range in Austria. On the left, the Röthbach waterfall tumbles 400m (1,312ft) into the lake. The Obersee is the starting point for numerous walks and hikes of varying difficulty, the most pleasant taking you around the lake to the Alpine region known as Fischunkel Alm in about 45 minutes.

Boat trips

In summer the boats depart from Königssee every 15 minutes, starting at 7.45am. In spring and autumn trips begin at 8.15am and the boats leave every 20 minutes. In winter they start at 9.45am, leaving every 45 minutes. Make sure you check the times of the last boat back.

For further information contact:
Bayerische Schifffahrt Königssee, Seestrasse 55, 83471 Schönau am Königssee.
Tel: (08652) 963 618;
www.seenschifffahrt.de

Tour: the Alpenstrasse

The Alpine Road (Deutsche Alpenstrasse) stretches from Lindau on the Bodensee (Lake Constance) to Berchtesgaden, a distance of nearly 300km (186 miles). Since this scenic route is too far to explore comfortably in one day, try touring just the easternmost part, starting at Grassau and driving along the B305 to Ramsau, just outside Berchtesgaden, a distance of 91km (57 miles), made exciting by hairpin bends and occasional 15 per cent gradients. For more information visit *www.german-alpine-road.com*

Start at Grassau, reached from Munich by taking the A8 autobahn southeast for about 78km (48 miles), then the B305 road south for 13km (8 miles).

1 Grassau

This holiday and health resort is dominated by the 1,586-m (5,203-ft)

high Hochplatte and boasts a late Gothic parish church with a Romanesque tower.

Drive 3km (2 miles) southeast along the B305 to Marquartstein.

2 Marquartstein

The composer Richard Strauss lived in

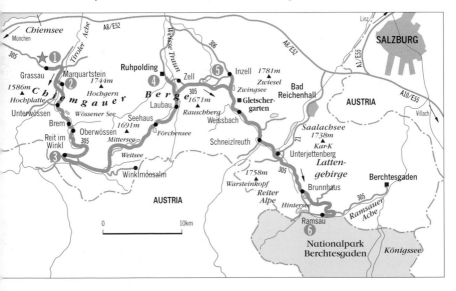

Bursagstrasse where he composed his opera *Salome*. Alongside the town's parish church is a signpost directing visitors to a nature park and a fairytale garden for children (Märchen-Erlebnispark).

Running in a southerly direction, the B305 now winds for 17km (11 miles) to Reit im Winkl.

3 Reit im Winkl

This Alpine holiday resort, on the Austrian border, flourishes in summer as well as in winter as ski lifts take visitors up to peaks that offer exhilarating panoramas.

Drive 24km (15 miles) northeast, through countryside dotted with lakes, to Ruhpolding.

4 Ruhpolding

A town of 7,000 inhabitants, Ruhpolding nonetheless preserves the charm of an Alpine village. The castle, built in 1597, houses a local history museum and there is a colourful 1930s Rathaus (Town Hall). The parish church of St George is one of the prettiest in the whole region, with a Romanesque façade and a mid-18th-century nave. The glory of the church is the Ruhpolding Madonna. Carved out of wood around 1230, she sits on the altar at the right-hand side of the apse. Ruhpolding's 17th-century cemetery chapel is also fascinating, with historic gravestones decorating the walls both inside and out. The town also has an amusement park (Märchen-Familienpark) with rides and much else besides to please the children.

Drive another 13km (8 miles) east to find Inzell.

5 Inzell

See pp80–81.
Next drive 34km (21 miles) southeast along the B305 to Ramsau.

6 Ramsau

This health and winter sports resort has a charming baroque pilgrimage church (Maria Kunterweg) that dates from 1733. The town's parish church was founded in the early 16th century and is like a scene from a Christmas card. Inside, old family names are set into personal pews. Gothic statues of Christ and the Apostles enhance the organ loft. The **Hintersee Lake**, 4km (2¹/₂ miles) westwards, is popular with anglers, swimmers and sailing enthusiasts.

Charming details arrest the eye in the town of Ruhpolding

Walk: around Inzell

This spectacular Alpine walk through beechwoods, pastures and stony mountain peaks is very demanding and should only be undertaken in summer and with proper walking shoes. The route is marked on the Wanderkarte map which is available from the tourist office in Inzell.

Allow 8 hours.

1 Inzell

Inzell is a delightful village, set in a valley with fine views of the mountains. The parish church of St Michael was founded by Archbishop Albrecht II of Salzburg in 1190. Most of this building was burned down in 1724, leaving only the Romanesque belfry, which supports a baroque onion dome. The new nave, begun three years after the fire, is beautifully decorated and has a splendid organ loft.

Opposite is the Rathaus, and there are plenty of good local inns, including the

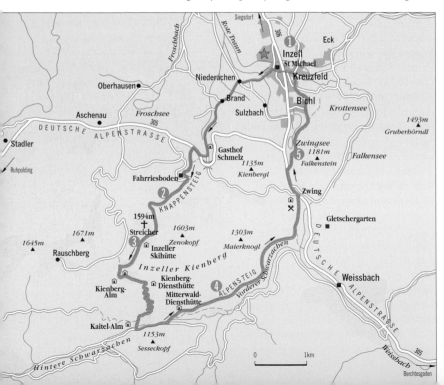

early 16th-century Gasthof zur Post.
Passing the parish church and graveyard,
take the road to Niederachen, walking
through Brand to reach the Gasthof
Schmelz. Turn right at the Gasthof,
crossing the main road, and look for a
narrow path that climbs steeply through
mountain woods to the chapel of
Fahrriesboden. Turn left here to walk for
some 200m (650ft) until you reach
a steep track (the Knappensteig) running
off to the right.

2 The Knappensteig

The Knappensteig brings you to the
entrance of several tunnels belonging to
a disused mine.
Next it crosses scree slopes and then makes
its way through pine trees. This is where
the route becomes extremely steep. You
will eventually reach a saddle offering
views of the mountains to the south. To
the right a cross crowns the nearest peak.

3 Mountain peaks

The view from the cross takes in such
peaks as the Watzmann, the Hochkalter,
the Hocheissspitze and the Reiter Alpe.
Close by is the Inzeller Skihütte, the ski-
hut of the Inzell sports club.
From the mountain cross
the route now runs

past the ski hut to Kienberg Alm, where
you turn left to reach the Kienberg
hunting lodge (the Kienberg Diensthütte).
Dizzily twisting southwards, the Alpine
road will now take you to Kaitel-Alm.

4 Alpensteig

At Kaitel-Alm, turn sharply left to hike
to the Alpensteig (Alpine Track) which
you follow until it eventually arrives at
Zwing. Here you can take a break to sip
tea in the Café Zwing.

5 Zwingsee

Turn north to walk through woods and
alongside the German Alpine Road
(Deutsche Alpenstrasse) as far as the
Zwingsee. The route runs around the
right-hand side of the lake. At the far side
of the lake keep walking northeasterly
and then turn northwards, hiking
through meadows lying at the foot of
the Falkenstein range, to reach Bichl.
Further north is Kreuzfeld, where you turn
left at the Gasthaus Falkenstein and walk
on under the Bundesstrasse back to Inzell.

The charming little village of Inzell
where this walk starts

Southwest Bavaria

Augsburg

The name of Augsburg, a city cooled by elaborate 16th-century fountains, indicates its antiquity, for the legions of the Roman Emperor Augustus founded a camp here where the Rivers Lech and Wertach meet. In the Middle Ages Augsburg became a city of wealthy bankers, in particular the Fugger family. Great artists, including Hans Holbein the Elder and his son Hans Holbein the Younger, lived and worked here. (For a walk round the town, *see pp96–7.*)

Dom St Maria (Cathedral)

Founded in 994, the oldest part of Augsburg's cathedral is the crypt. Inside there are four paintings by Hans Holbein the Elder and five stained-glass windows (in the south clerestory) dating from the 12th century and the oldest in Germany. On the south side are Romanesque bronze doors decorated with 35 reliefs depicting scenes from the Old Testament.
Frauentorstrasse 1. Open: 9am–5.30pm.

One of Augsburg's many fountains

Fuggerei

These almshouses were founded in 1516 by Jakob Fugger 'the Rich'.
Mittlere Gasse 13. Open: Mar–23 Dec, daily 9am–6pm. Closed: Jan & Feb.

Maximilianmuseum

The Augsburg gold and silver collection is one of this local history museum's many highlights.
Philippine-Welser-Strasse 24. Open: Tue–Sun 10am–5pm. Admission charge.

Rathausplatz

The city's main square centres on the Augustus fountain, created by Hubert Gerhard in 1588 to celebrate the 1600th anniversary of the founding of the city. It features a statue of Emperor Augustus and symbols of the four rivers that flow through the region. To one side of the square is Elias Holl's Renaissance town hall completed in 1620. Its Golden Hall has a superb coffered ceiling and wall paintings. The Perlachturm, rising alongside Peterskirche, offers fine views from the top.
Golden Hall open: daily 10am–6pm. Perlachturm open: May–mid-Oct, daily 10am–6pm.

St Ulrich-und-Afra

Founded in 1474, this late Gothic basilica is crammed with Renaissance and baroque works of art.
Maximilianstrasse. Open: 9am–5.30pm.

Schaezlerpalais

The palace displays three important art collections, including that of the

Augsburg (*see walk on pp96–7 for route*)

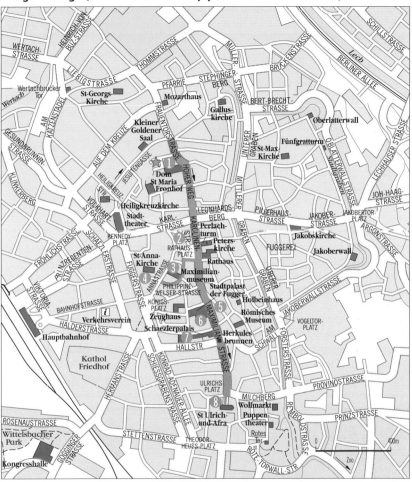

Staatsgalerie with works by Lukas Cranach the Elder and Albrecht Dürer. *Maximilianstrasse 46. Open: Tue–Sun 10am–4pm.*

Augsburg is 50km (31 miles) northwest of Munich. Tourist office: Regio Augsburg Tourismus, Bahnhofstrasse 7. Tel: (0821) 502 0735; www.augsburg-tourismus.de

Augsburg Zoo

Augsburg Zoo is set in 22ha (54 acres) of parkland on the borders of the Siebentisch forest and features over 2,000 animals and birds from all over the world.
Tel: (0821) 555031; www.zoo-augsburg.de. Open: daily 9am–6.30pm; to 5pm in winter. Bus: 32 from Augsburg Central Station to Zoo/Botanischer Garten. Admission charge.

Ettal

In 1327, Ludwig the Bavarian, Duke of Bavaria and Holy Roman Emperor, made a pilgrimage to Rome where he bought a statue of the Virgin Mary. On the return journey the emperor's horse stopped at Ettal (so the legend runs) and genuflected to the statue. This inspired Ludwig to found a splendid Benedictine monastery here with an unusual 12-sided abbey church, modelled on the Church of the Holy Sepulchre in Jerusalem.

Most of the old abbey (though not the statue of the Virgin Mary) was destroyed in a fire of 1744. In rebuilding the church, the Italian Enrico Zuccalli, assisted by the Bavarian Franz Xavier Schmuzer, created one of Bavaria's finest rococo buildings. His church, which retains the 12-sided pattern of its predecessor, is surmounted by a dome designed by Schmuzer, and the interior is frescoed with 431 figures glorifying the Benedictine order of monks. The high altar enshrines the statue brought by Ludwig the Bavarian from Rome, and

Johann Baptist Zimmermann contributed an inspired pink-and-white rococo organ loft and organ case.
70km (43 miles) south of Munich, 6km (4 miles) southeast of Oberammergau. Tourist office: Ammergauer Strasse 8. Tel: (08822) 3534; fax: (08822) 6399; www.ettal.de. For information about the monastery and its excellent beer, visit www.kloster-ettal.de

Füssen

Füssen grew up around an 8th-century monastery founded to enshrine the bones of St Mang (or Magnus). The original abbey has, for the most part, been superseded by 18th-century baroque buildings created by Johann Jakob Herkomer (though the crypt remains 11th-century). Today, it houses the local history museum. Close by, and picturesquely set on a hill, is the Hohes Schloss. This was built in 1322 for the Prince-Bishop of Augsburg, enlarged by Bishop Friedrich von Zollern around 1500 and extended again in the 19th

Ettal's 12-sided abbey church

Southwest Bavaria

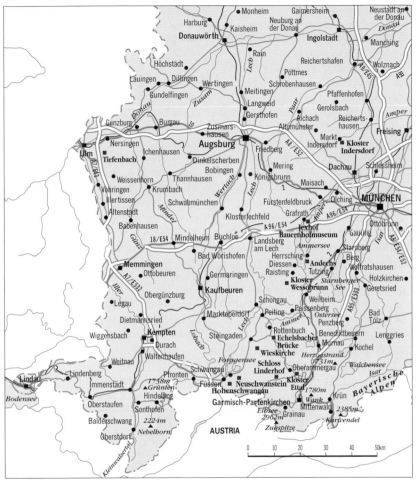

century for King Maximilian I. The Gothic chapel has a fine Coronation of the Virgin, painted around 1500. The east wing, added in the early 14th century, encompasses the Knights' Hall with its 16th-century coffered ceiling. The north wing displays paintings from the Bavarian national collection.

Both the history museum and the Hohes Schloss are open: summer, Tue–Sun 11am–4pm; winter, 2–4pm.

Füssen is 120km (75 miles) southwest of Munich. Tourist office: Kaiser-Maximilian Platz 1. Tel: (08362) 93850; fax: (08362) 938 620; www.fuessen.de

Garmisch-Partenkirchen

The twin towns of Garmisch and Partenkirchen together form one of Germany's most popular resorts, beautifully sited at the foot of the Alps. The 1936 winter Olympics were held here, and the 1978 world skiing championships. As a result the town has become a premier winter sports centre, with an Olympic ski-jump and ice stadium. Garmisch-Partenkirchen also remains a haven for hikers in summer. Several of the nearby peaks are accessible by cable car or rack railway, including Germany's highest mountain, Zugspitze (2,962m/9,718ft), Wank (1,780m/5,840ft) and Eckbauer (1,237m/4,058ft). Close to the town is the beautiful Partnachklamm gorge, dubbed one of 'the Wonders of the World'. It is reached on foot or by means of a horse and carriage from the Olympic ice stadium along a 2-km (1¼-mile) road (cars are banned). A path runs through the gorge which is remarkably narrow and deep, with a number of unusual rock formations. Another popular sight is the tiny Lake Badersee, in the little village of Grainau, just west of Garmisch-Partenkirchen. Boats can be hired here that will take you to see the statue of the water nymph, Nixe, placed at the bottom of the lake by King Ludwig II.

120km (75 miles) southwest of Munich. Tourist office: Richard-Strauss-Platz 2. Tel: (08821) 180 700; fax: (08821) 180 450; www.garmisch-partenkirchen.de

Immenstadt

Immenstadt is an enticing little Alpine town and a fine centre for skiing and hiking (with marked routes). It is conveniently close to the Grosser Alpsee lake which in summer is used for watersports. The ambience is enhanced by the surrounding mountains, dominated by the 1,738-m (5,702-ft) high Grünten.

149km (93 miles) southwest of Munich, 55km (34 miles) east of Lindau. Tourist office: in the Rathaus on

The flowerbeds and buildings in Kempten

The twin towns of Garmisch and Partenkirchen lie beneath Zugspitze's peaks

Marienplatz. Tel: (08323) 914 176;
fax: (08323) 914 195; www.immenstadt.de

Kempten

Kempten is a busy commercial town
with a number of good museums
devoted to archaeology and local
history. They include the Alpenmuseum
(Alpine Museum) and the
Zumsteinhaus, a fine classical building
of 1802 used to display archaeological
finds from the site of the original
Roman town of Cambodunum; the
latter stands at the centre of an
archaeological park to the east of town,
across the River Iller.
Museums open: Tue–Sun 10am–4pm.
Archaeological park open: May–Oct,
Tue–Sun 10am–5pm, Nov, Dec, Mar &
Apr until 4.30pm. Closed: Jan & Feb.
Kempten is 124km (77 miles) southwest
of Munich.
Tourist office: Rathausplatz 24.
Tel: (0831) 252 5237; fax: (0831) 252
5427; www.kempten.de

Kleinwalsertal

This exquisite valley is overlooked by the
bizarrely shaped rocks of the Widderstein
(which rises to 2,533m/8,310ft) and
such dramatic peaks as the Grünhorn
(2,039m/6,690ft) and the Hoher Ifen
(2,230m/7,316ft). Oddly enough, the
valley belongs to Austria but can only be
entered from Bavaria (you do not need
to show a passport when crossing the
border). As in Germany, local currency
is the euro, though its vehicles bear

Austrian number plates. This is a paradise not only for hikers but also for winter sports fanatics, and the valley's three major towns are all entrancing. The facilities at Riezlern include a casino and dance-cafés. At Hirschegg there is a pleasant theatre, swimming pools, sauna, golf and bowling courses, and tennis courts. Mittelberg has a baroque church, and some of the 18th-century houses have painted façades. There is also a pleasant public garden, the Kurpark in Riezlern.

190km (118 miles) southwest of Munich, 55km (34 miles) south of Kempten.
Tourist office: Im Walserhaus, Hirschegg.
Tel: (08329) 51140; fax: (08329) 511 421;
e-mail: info@kleinwalsertal.com

Landsberg am Lech

If you are visiting this lovely hillside town, you can follow the well-signposted town walk, the Stadtrundgang, which will take you down characterful alleys to the town's 15th-century walls, from where there are good views of the River Lech. A free walk map can be collected from the tourist office in the main square, Hauptplatz. Here, too, you can see the superb Rathaus (Town Hall) with its rich stucco façade designed by one of Bavaria's finest architects, Domenikus Zimmermann, who served as the town's Bürgermeister (Mayor) between 1759 and 1764. Also worth seeing is the 16th-century stained glass in the choir of the Maria Himmelfahrt church.

54km (33 miles) west of Munich.
Tourist office: Hauptplatz 1.
Tel: (08191) 128 246; e-mail:
fremdenverkehrsamt@landsberg.de

Lindau

Lindau sits on an island at the east end of the Bodensee, better known as Lake Constance, the second largest of the Alpine lakes (after Lake Geneva). Lindau's harbour is home to a fleet of boats that carry visitors round the 65-km (40-mile) long lake, which forms the border between Bavaria and Austria. The harbour is guarded by a statue of the heraldic Lion of Bavaria and two lighthouses – one dating from the 13th century and once part of the city's fortifications, the other from 1865.

The town has delightful traffic-free lakeside promenades, while its Altstadt (old town) is lined by attractive medieval and baroque houses. At St Peter's Church you can see the only surviving frescoes by Hans Holbein the Elder, dating from the 1480s.

Tourist office: Ludwigstrasse 68.
Tel: (08382) 260 030; fax: (08382) 260 026; www.lindau-tourismus.de

Linderhof

Of the three castles built by King Ludwig II (*see pp94–5*), Linderhof is the most endearing because of its lovely formal gardens and its woodland setting. Ludwig intended the castle as a 'new Versailles' but the original lavish scheme was never realised. Instead this fine Rococo villa was built, with its Hall of Mirrors and its extraordinary dining table, designed to be lowered to the kitchen below and hoisted back up laden with dishes full of food. In the garden is the Venus Grotto (*closed in winter*), an artificial cave that Wagner used to stage his opera, *Tannhäuser*. Germany's first ever electric lighting scheme was devised

to illuminate the cave's waterfall and lake.
*100km (62 miles) southwest of Munich,
20km (12 miles) southwest of
Oberammergau. Open: daily, summer
9am–6pm, until 8pm on Thur; winter
10am–4pm. Admission charge.*

Oberammergau

Home of Germany's celebrated Passion
Play (*see pp90–91*), Oberammergau is
also a typically beautiful Alpine village.
That beauty is enhanced by the work of
the 18th-century local artist Franz
Joseph Zwinck, who developed to
perfection the art of *trompe l'oeil*
painting and decorated several houses in
the town with scenes giving the illusion
of three-dimensional columned halls
and swirling steps. Many shops in the
town sell locally carved wooden figures,
mostly on religious themes, and there
is a display of historic Christmas cribs
in the local history museum on
Dorfstrasse.

You can also visit the Passion Play
Theatre. This is a severely functional
building but the acoustics are perfect.
Backstage is an informative exhibition of
costumes and props used in the Passion
Play.

More spectacular is the parish church
of St Peter and St Paul, by the rococo
architect Joseph Schmuzer. He designed
the double organ loft and painted the
third (*trompe l'oeil*) loft above it. In the
great dome Matthäus Günther painted
the martyrdoms of St Peter and St Paul
and their entry into the heavenly
Jerusalem. Franz Xavier Schmädl
sculpted the pulpit and the magnificent
high altar with its drapery, up and down
which a host of cherubs flies.

The cemetery contains the graves of
Alois Daisenberger, the pastor to whom
Oberammergau owes the present form
of its Passion Play, and Rochus Dedler,
who composed its music.
*100km (62 miles) southwest of Munich.
Tourist office: Eugen-Papst-Strasse 9a.
Tel: (0822) 92310; fax: (0822) 923 190;
www.oberammergau.de.
History museum open: 15 May–15 Oct
Tue–Sun 2–6pm; rest of year Sat only.
Admission charge. Passion Play Theatre
open: May–Oct 9.30am–noon & 1–4pm,
Nov–Apr 10am–noon & 1–4pm.*

The gorgeous Hall of Mirrors at Linderhof Castle,
one of several lavish rooms

Passion Play

Although plagues were endemic in 17th-century Bavaria, the Thirty Years' War made them even more frequent, with marauding armies spreading the disease. The war was in its 14th year when the epidemic reached Oberammergau in 1632, brought by an infected man from nearby Eschenlohe who crept into the village at night, evading the guards set to keep strangers out. By the end of the year, the disease had killed 84 villagers.

The following July, all those who were still able to walk processed to the parish church and solemnly vowed that if God lifted the plague, they would perform a Passion Play every ten years, recounting the events of Holy Week from Christ's triumphant entry into Jerusalem on Palm Sunday to the Crucifixion and subsequent Resurrection. From that moment, no other villager died of the disease. So 1634 saw the first performance of the Passion Play, 1644 the second. As time passed, the play began to be performed at the turn of each decade, so that the next performances will take place in 2010.

Initially, the citizens of Oberammergau borrowed a play written earlier by the monks of Augsburg. Today the play is essentially that written by Oberammergau's mid-19th-century parish priest, Alois Daisenberger. It is accompanied by the baroque music composed for earlier performances by Rochus

Dedler (born in Oberammergau in 1799). Another remarkable feature is the 'Living Tableaux' – episodes from the Old Testament in which the scene, though crowded with actors, is motionless, an event frozen in time.

As always, the Passion Play is performed solely by those born in the village, and competition for the major parts is very keen. Nowadays so many visitors come to see the play that each of the main roles is given to two actors who perform on alternate days throughout the Passion Play season. The play, which takes all day to perform, involves a cast of 1,700 and is seen by over half a million people during the 100-day season.

Villagers prepare for years for the Oberammergau Passion Play

Early-morning mist in Schwangau

Ottobeuren

Ottobeuren is the site of one of
Germany's largest churches, a mighty
baroque building with a 90-m (295-ft)
long nave. It was built to serve the
town's Benedictine abbey, originally
founded in 764, which prospered under
the patronage of the Holy Roman
Emperor, Charlemagne. The church was
rebuilt in 1737 by Johann Michael
Fischer, and several other major artists
contributed to the light and airy
cathedral-like interior with its fine
frescoes and splendid organ. Near to
Ottobeuren is the large town of
Memmingen, with its attractive
medieval centre and the splendid Gothic
spire of St Martinskirche.
120km (75 miles) west of Munich.
Tourist office: Marktplatz 14, Ottobeuren.
Tel: (08332) 921 950/921 992.

Schwangau

Schwangau is a quite charming rustic
village, famous principally as a base for
visiting the splendid royal castles of
Hohenschwangau and Neuschwanstein.
Both castles enjoy a spectacular setting
against the backdrop of Alpine crags,
but both can also be very crowded.

Hohenschwangau

Hohenschwangau, the lower and older
of the two castles, rises on the spot
where a stronghold of the Knights of the
Swan stood from the 12th century until
Napoleon Bonaparte demolished it.
In 1832, the future King Maximilian II
commissioned the theatre architect
Dominik Quaglio to recreate a medieval
dream castle here. After Quaglio's death
in 1837, Joseph Daniel Ohlmüller and
GF Ziebland finished the work.

The 14 rooms that are open to visitors
glorify the Wittelsbach dynasty. Statues
of Emperor Ludwig the Bavarian and
Elector Maximilian I flank the entrance.
The deeds of Germany's medieval heroes
are portrayed in frescoes commissioned
from Moritz von Schwind and Wilhelm
Lindenschmidt. Here, too, are portraits
of Charlemagne and Martin Luther.
Richard Wagner (*see pp118–19*) often
stayed at Hohenschwangau, and his
opera *Lohengrin* inspired the decoration
of the Hall of the Knights of the Swan:
here, the seats and the huge silver
chandelier have swan motifs and the
centrepiece is another silver swan, a
wedding present from the citizens of
Munich to Maximilian.

Hohenschwangau is filled with
oddities, none more so than the
Queen's Bedroom, which is in the
Turkish style (a consequence of
Maximilian's visit to Turkey in 1833)
and furnished with settees given by
Sultan Muhammed II. Another curiosity
is the bedroom of Maximilian's son, the
future Ludwig II, which is decorated
with stars that could be lit up
dramatically in the evening when the
prince retired for the night.

Neuschwanstein

Neuschwanstein is the splendid creation of King Ludwig II. Though unfinished at the time of his mysterious death (only 15 out of a projected 65 rooms were built), it remains one of the world's most stunningly romantic fairytale castles. Part of a mountain peak was blasted away to provide it with a solid base, and to reach the castle involves a hard uphill climb – you can take a bus, or opt for a more romantic horse-drawn carriage from the car park.

Ludwig commissioned the architects Eduard Riedl, Georg Dollmann and Julius Hofmann to create this masterpiece of fantasy and pseudo-medievalism. Throughout there are references to the unreal world of Wagner's operas. The decoration of the entrance hall was inspired by the *Nibelungen* cycle; the dining room and the king's study are painted with scenes from *Tannhäuser*; Ludwig's living room and bedroom display scenes from *Tristan and Isolde*; the décor of the Sängersaal (Singers' Hall) was inspired by *Parsifal*, and the upper courtyard is based on an 1867 set designed for *Lohengrin*.

Neuschwanstein displays remarkable feats of engineering and artistry, with its winding staircases, columns sculpted like palm trees, and its Byzantine throne room with a golden chandelier weighing 900kg (1,984lb) and a marble floor incorporating over 2.5 million pieces. Equally enthralling are the vistas of the Bavarian Alps and of nearby lakes that reveal themselves through the windows. *Both castles open: summer 9am–6pm, until 8pm on Thur, winter 10am–4pm. Guided tours daily in summer. Admission charge. Tickets are only available at the Ticket-Service Hohenschwangau, Alpseestrasse 12. Tel: (08362) 930 830.*

Schwangau is 120km (75 miles) southwest of Munich.
Tourist office: Münchener Strasse 2.
Tel: (08362) 81980; fax: (08362) 819 825;
www.schwangau.de

A pensive monarch considers the deeds of German heroes at Hohenschwangau

In August 1845, a long-awaited heir to the Bavarian throne was born. Christened Ludwig, he spent most of his childhood in romantic isolation at Hohenschwangau (*see p92*) where, at the age of 16, he became enraptured by the music of Richard Wagner (*see p118*).

In 1864, he was crowned King Ludwig II. If his friendship with Wagner brought him enemies, his foreign policy made him even more detested, for he supported his ministers in a war against Prussia that ended in ignominious defeat after only three weeks, and Bavaria was forced to pay the Prussians 50 million marks in gold as a penalty. When the Franco-Prussian War of 1870 broke out, Ludwig and his ministers made the wiser decision to side with Prussia.

In the meantime, he spent lavish sums building his dream castles: Schloss Herrenchiemsee (*see p67*), Schloss Neuschwanstein (*p93*) and Schloss Linderhof (*pp88–9*). All three are replete

with references to two of Ludwig's idols, Richard Wagner and French King Louis XIV.

Herrenchiemsee is virtually a replica of Versailles, the palace of Louis XIV, while the French king's motto *Nec pluribus impar* is embossed on the ceilings at Linderhof and there are statues of Louis XIV in the entrance hall and the garden. Linderhof also exhibits examples of Ludwig's eccentric lifestyle: the table in the dining room could be cranked up to Ludwig so that he could eat alone without ever seeing his servants.

Ludwig spent his own private fortune on his castles and got the state deeply into debt. His alarmed ministers persuaded doctors to declare the king insane, forcing him to abdicate and to submit to house arrest at Schloss Berg, a castle beside the Starnberg Lake. On Whitsunday 1886 his body, along with that of his physician Dr von Gudden, were discovered mysteriously drowned in the lake. To this day it remains a mystery whether Ludwig died accidentally or deliberately – whether he committed suicide or was murdered.

Equally, the world remains divided as to whether Ludwig was a misunderstood genius or simply mad. In any event, the castles he once built at great cost have now repaid the investment many times over in revenue from the millions of visitors who come to see them every year.

Facing page: ceiling detail (below) and the dining room at Schloss Linderhof
This page: the concert hall (below left) and the King's study, Schloss Neuschwanstein

Walk: Augsburg

This walk shows you the main sights of Augsburg, Bavaria's oldest city, founded in the reign of Augustus, the first Roman emperor, in the 1st century BC (*see map on p83 for the route*).

Allow 2 hours.

Begin at the Domkirche.

1 Dom St Maria (Cathedral)
Of particular interest in this cathedral are the four altarpieces painted by Hans Holbein the Elder, and also the five stained-glass windows in the nave depicting Old Testament prophets. (*see also p82*).

From here take Hoher Weg and Karolinenstrasse to Rathausplatz.

2 Rathausplatz
The town-hall square has a fine late 16th-century fountain with statues representing the Emperor Augustus and four of the region's rivers. Nearby, the Perlachturm began life as an 11th-century watchtower but was raised to more than 70m (230ft) in height by Elias Holl in 1616. It houses a 35-bell glockenspiel that chimes daily at noon. Behind the Perlachturm rises the 12th-century Romanesque Peterskirche, the Church of St Peter. Behind the Rathaus (*see p82*), in Elias-Holl-Platz, is Die Ecke, an inn founded in 1492.

With your back to the Rathaus, cross Rathausplatz to the traffic-free shopping area around Philippine-Welser-Strasse and Annastrasse. At Philippine-Welser-Strasse 24 is the Maximilianmuseum.

3 Maximilianmuseum
This important local history museum is situated in two impressive Renaissance buildings from the late 15th and mid-16th centuries. In over 30 rooms it presents exhibits relating to the city's illustrious history, along with sculptures and local arts and crafts. Highlights include a large collection of gold and silver smithery, and works by the early baroque sculptors Adriaen de Vries and Georg Petel.

Continue through Martin-Luther-Platz to Annastrasse.

4 St-Anna-Kirche
This Gothic church, founded in 1321, gave shelter to Luther in 1518 after whom the Lutherhof cloister of 1521 is named. Its highlights are the Goldsmith's chapel, built in the 1420s and still preserving 15th-century wall paintings, and the Renaissance funeral chapel that Hans Burkmaier created for the Fuggers between 1508 and 1519.

Retrace your steps to Maximilianstrasse.

5 Maximilianstrasse
Cobbled Maximilianstrasse threads through the heart of the St Anna district, following the course of the Roman Via Claudia. It is one of the

finest (and certainly one of the longest-surviving) medieval streets in Europe.

6 Stadtpalast der Fugger

At Maximilianstrasse 36 you will find the Fugger Palace, built between 1512 and 1515 for Jakob Fugger. It incorporates a lovely arcaded interior, frescoed by Hans Burkmaier, and Elias Holl's Zeughaus (Arsenal), built in 1607 and his first job as Augsburg's city architect.

Further south is the fine Herkulesbrunnen (Hercules Fountain), made between 1596 and 1602. Opposite stands the most sumptuous baroque building in the city, the Schaezlerpalais.

7 Schaezlerpalais

This magnificent rococo palace was built for the Augsburg banker Benedikt von Liebenhofen in the 18th century. Today it houses three significant art collections, each of which alone would justify a visit. The Stiftung Haberstock contains works by the Venetian painters Canaletto and Veronese, in the Baroque Gallery are important works from the 17th and 18th centuries, and in the Staatsgalerie (State Art Gallery) you can admire paintings by such great masters as Lukas Cranach the Elder, Hans Holbein the Elder and Albrecht Dürer. It is above all the latter collection that helps to illustrate the incredible prosperity this former free imperial city enjoyed between the 15th and 17th centuries, as it emphasises not only paintings gathered from Augsburg's churches, but also artworks that are closely connected with the city's history, for instance Dürer's portrait of the

Augsburg banker Jakob Fugger 'the Rich' (1459–1525).

The street continues to Ulrichsplatz and the basilica of St Ulrich und Afra.

8 St Ulrich-und-Afra

Built on the site of a Roman temple, this church was founded by Kaiser Maximilian I in 1474 and built by Burkhardt Engelberg between 1476 and 1500 (*see p82*). It shelters many Fugger family tombs, as well as the relics of both its patron saints. St Ulrich lies in a rococo tomb. The asymmetrical tower of the basilica was topped with an onion dome around 1600, and this set the fashion that is now typical of Bavarian church architecture.

Elias Holl's magnificent Renaissance Rathaus in Rathausplatz

Central Bavaria

Ansbach

Set amidst the forests of the Rezat Valley, Ansbach is the venue of an international Bach festival held every odd-numbered year at the end of July.

Markgrafenschloss

Ansbach was ruled by the Margraves of Brandenburg-Ansbach, for whom this splendid palace was built in the first half of the 18th century. Inside you will find a double-storeyed Great Hall, exuberantly frescoed by Christian Carlone, and a hall of mirrors containing some superb porcelain figures. The surrounding parkland contains stately avenues of lime trees laid out some 250 years ago. There is also a fine baroque orangery built in 1736. In the garden there is a memorial to the so-called 'wolf-boy', Kaspar Hauser, a foundling discovered wandering in Nürnberg in 1828, who was murdered here in mysterious circumstances.

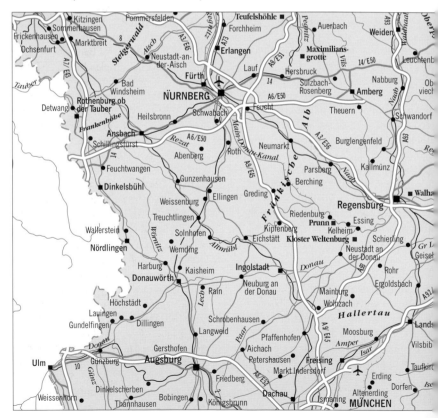

*Open: summer, Tue–Sun 9am–noon &
1–5pm; winter 10am–noon & 1–3pm.
Admission charge.*

St Gumbert

St Gumbert shelters the tombs of 11
Knights of the Swan (an order founded
by Elector Friedrich II of Brandenburg
in 1440). The altar of the Order of the
Swan was carved by Martin Wohlgemut
or his pupils in 1484. The Romanesque
crypt and the funeral vault has 25 tombs
of the Margraves and their relatives.
Open: 9am–5.30pm.

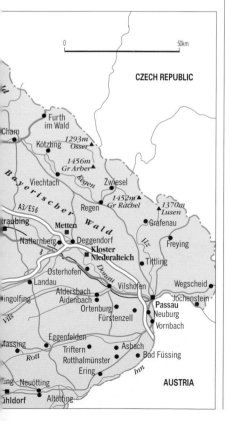

*Ansbach is 165km (103 miles) northwest
of Munich, 55km (34 miles) southwest of
Nürnberg. Tourist office: Johann-
Sebastian-Bach-Platz 1. Tel: (0981)
51243; fax: (0981) 51365;
www.ansbach.de*

Dinkelsbühl

Dinkelsbühl is a gem of a town on the
Romantische Strasse (the Romantic
Road – *see pp110–11*), set within a ring
of picturesque walls around which you
can stroll, just as the town's
nightwatchman does every evening.

Martin Luther Strasse, the town's
main street, leads to Marktplatz with the
15th-century parish church of St
George. This is one of Bavaria's grandest
churches, with a resplendent late Gothic
fan vault soaring high above the nave.
*150km (93 miles) northwest of Munich,
83km (52 miles) southwest of Nürnberg.
Tourist office: Marktplatz. Tel: (09851)
90240; fax: (09851) 90279;
www.dinkelsbuehl.de*

Donauwörth

Beautifully situated at the point where
the River Wörnitz joins the Danube, this
town has two medieval gateways and
several elegant streets, the finest of
which is the Reichsstrasse. Dominating
Reichsstrasse is the huge tower of the
Church of Our Lady. The mid-15th-
century church has frescoes and stained-
glass windows of the same date, and a
stone tabernacle carved around 1600.
Nearby is the Fuggerhaus, a patrician
home built in 1539 by Anton Fugger at
the corner of Heilig-Kreuz-Strasse and
Pflegerstrasse. Deutschordenshaus,
formerly a commandery of the Teutonic

Knights, was built at the end of the 18th century. On the first floor is a beautifully decorated banquet hall known as the Enderlesaal, and also the municipal art gallery.

90km (56 miles) northwest of Munich, 37km (23 miles) north of Augsburg. Tourist office: Rathausgasse 1. Tel: (0906) 789 151; fax: (0906) 789 999.

Eichstätt

The great cathedral church in Eichstätt was founded by the missionary St Willibald in AD 740. Built in a mixture of Romanesque, Gothic and baroque, it houses the famous Pappenheim altar, a huge medieval depiction of the Crucifixion. In the Willibald choir, you can see the tomb of the missionary saint with its movingly realistic carving of St Willibald portrayed in old age.

The town's other main sight is the Willibaldsburg, the huge fortress palace built by the Prince-Bishops who ruled from 1355 until 1755. It houses two natural history museums, one of which (the Jura-Museum) contains the fossilised bones of the primitive bird archaeopteryx. In the Pre- and Early History Museum are skeletons of a mammoth and cave hyenas.

90km (56 miles) northwest of Munich, 28km (17 miles) north of Ingolstadt. Tourist office: Domplatz 8. Tel: (08421) 98800; fax: (08421) 988 030. Museums open: Apr–Sept, Tue–Sun 9am–5pm; Oct–Mar 10am–4pm.

The cathedral city of Eichstätt

Ingolstadt

Still guarded by the triple walls of its early 15th-century fortifications and by the Kreuztor of 1383, Ingolstadt lies picturesquely beside the River Danube. The city's cathedral of Our Lady, the Liebfrauenkirche, is a massive brick building finished in 1520. Entered by a flamboyant Gothic south porch, it boasts exuberantly carved choir stalls and pulpit, as well as late 15th- and early 16th-century stained glass. Later in date is the baroque Asam-Kirche Maria de Viktoria, whose ceiling, frescoed by Cosmas Damian Asam, is a masterpiece of perspective. Johann Michael Fischer created its magnificent high altar, which has statues representing medicine, theology, mathematics and philosophy.

Memories of the city's importance as a garrison town on the Danube are evoked by the Paradeplatz, laid out for military displays and overlooked by the moated Herzogschloss, founded by Duke Ludwig the Bearded in 1418. The castle now serves as the **Bavarian Army Museum**.

In Rathausplatz, you will find the hospice church, the Spitalkirche, founded by Ludwig the Bavarian in 1319. In the same square are the city's twin town halls, one dating from 1592, the other created from four Gothic houses in 1882. Behind the town hall, in Moritzstrasse, stands the Gothic church of St Moritz, with a silver Madonna by Ignaz Günther and stucco work by Johann Baptist Zimmermann.
75km (47 miles) northwest of Munich. Tourist office: Rathausplatz 2. Tel: (0841) 305 1098; fax: (0841) 305 1099; www.ingolstadt-tourist.de

Massive towers in Ingolstadt recall the town's military role as a Danube garrison

Army Museum open: daily (except Mon) 8.45am–4.30pm. Admission charge.

Nördlingen

Nördlingen is the capital of the area known as the 'Ries', a circular crater some 25km (16 miles) in diameter created by a meteorite which crashed here some 15 million years ago. The city is protected by circular ramparts, built in the 14th century, five gates and 16 towers.

The almost perfect circle that defines the city of Nördlingen clearly seen from up high

The finest view of Nördlingen, and of the surrounding Ries, is from the 90-m (295-ft) high tower of the church of St George. The tower is nicknamed 'Daniel' and there are 365 steps to the copper dome at the summit, added in 1539. Opposite the church of St George is the half-timbered Tanzhaus, a building of the 1440s formerly used by the drapers for selling their goods during Nördlingen's Whitsun fairs, which drew traders from all over Germany. The statue placed over the entrance in 1513 represents Emperor Maximilian I, an orb in his right hand, his left hand resting on his sword.

Exquisite 16th- and 17th-century houses – some half-timbered, others baroque – ring the medieval heart of the city, situated around the Marktplatz. Here you will find the Rathaus, Nördlingen's town hall. This was built in the 13th and 14th centuries and was initially the venue for the town's Whitsun Fair. In 1618 Wolfgang Wallberger added its magnificent open staircase.

To find out more about the town you can visit the Stadtmuseum, housed in the 16th-century hospice of the Holy Ghost.

100km (62 miles) northwest of Munich. Tourist office: Marktplatz 2. Tel: (09081) 84116; fax: (09081) 84113; www.noerdlingen.de. Stadmuseum open: Mar–Oct, Tue–Sun 1.30–4.30pm.

Circular ramparts, with circular towers, ring the heart of medieval Nördlingen

Nürnberg

Nürnberg (Nuremberg in English) was one of the great medieval cities of Germany, and after heavy bombing during World War II it was rebuilt to preserve the best of the former city within the modern one. Eighty towers rise from the city walls, whose outer ring dates from 1400, and irregular streets lead down to ancient bridges over the River Pegnitz.

Characterful Nürnberg, birthplace of Dürer, has risen from the ashes of war

Dürer-Haus

Albrecht Dürer (1471–1528), one of the finest Renaissance artists of Northern Europe, bought this house in 1509 and lived here for the rest of his life. Here he created many of his superb engravings (including charming and naturalistic depictions of rabbits). The museum in the house is devoted to Dürer's work.
Albrecht-Dürer-Strasse 39.
Tel: (0911) 231 2568. Open: Tue–Sun 9.30am–6pm, Thur until 8pm.
Admission charge.

Hauptmarkt

Every weekday, local farmers from the area around Nürnberg come to the city to sell their produce in the Hauptmarkt, the main market square. Another attraction is the cathedral clock with its 16th-century figures of the seven German Electors of Germany who pay homage to the Holy Roman Emperor. Nearby stands Nürnberg's greatest fountain, the triple-tiered Schöner Brunnen, which was created by Heinrich Parler. Among its 40 figures are nine Old Testament heroes, the Four Evangelists, Charlemagne, King Arthur, and the four Fathers of the Church.

Kaiserburg

The imperial castle was built between 1167 and 1495 and was the home of the emperors till 1571. All that one imagines in a medieval castle is here, including a 13th-century keep and a 53-m (174-ft) deep well. The terrace gives a superb view. *Kaiserburgmuseum open: Apr–Sept, daily 9am–6pm; Oct–Mar, daily 10am–4pm. Guided tours: first Sat of every month at 2.30pm.*
Admission charge.

Museums

Nürnberg has numerous museums to suit all interests. The Germanisches Nationalmuseum is packed with works of art, including masterpieces by Cranach and Dürer. The Spielzeugmuseum has the world's biggest and most varied collection of historic toys, appropriate for a city that was regarded as the toy-manufacturing capital of Europe until World War II. Railway lovers should visit the Verkehrsmuseum (Transport Museum) to see Germany's first steam locomotive, the *Adler*. Opened in 2000, the Neues Museum displays international design

and applied art, along with modern art from the 1960s to the present day.
For details contact the tourist office, or www.museen.nuernberg.de

Nazi Party rally grounds
The grounds and excellent Documentation Centre provide a fascinating and forthright view of this era in Nürnberg's tumultuous history.
Bayernstrasse 110. Tel: (0911) 869 897. Open: Tue–Sun 10am–6pm. Take S-Bahn from the Hauptbahnhof to Frankenstadion. Admission charge.

St Lorenz
One of the few Nürnberg churches to survive the bombing of World War II, the 13th-century building, with its twin spires, contains two outstanding masterpieces: Adam Kraft's massive tabernacle (1493) and a carving of the

Annunciation (1517) by Veit Stoss (*see p128*). Opposite, the Nassauer Haus is a good example of a 13th-century residential building.
Lorenzerplatz. Open: 9am–5.30pm.

St Sebald
On Rathausplatz, Nürnberg's cathedral (13th-century) contains the bronze and silver shrine of St Sebald, an outstanding work of art created by Peter Vischer and his sons. Guides will point out where Peter Vischer has sculpted his own self-portrait on the tomb.
Open: 9am–5.30pm.

Nürnberg is 170km (106 miles) north of Munich. Tourist office: Königstrasse 93. Tel: (0911) 233 6132. There is also an office at Hauptmarkt 18. Tel: (0911) 233 6135; www.tourismus-nuernberg.de

Playful Bacchic figures revel amongst the spray at Nürnberg's Schöner Brunnen Fountain

Regensburg

This city on the Danube emerged from World War II remarkably unscathed and in consequence it has over 1,400 medieval buildings. You could spend hours exploring its churches and its alleys lined with Italianate tower houses and stately mansions. Now a university town with 135,000 inhabitants, Regensburg welcomes visitors to explore its patrician houses, churches and galleries, and to join its citizens in skimming the Danube in canoes and motor boats.

Altes Rathaus (Reichstagsmuseum)

Regensburg's former town hall, in Rathausplatz, was begun in 1360 and has a baroque east wing, plus a Venus fountain in its courtyard, both dating from 1661.

Rathausplatz 1. Guided tours of the Reichstags-museum (historic interior of the Rathaus): Apr–Oct every half hour, Mon–Sat 9.30am–noon & 2–4pm, Sun 10am–noon & 2–4pm. Otherwise every hour, Mon–Sat 9.30–11.30am & 2–4pm, Sun 10am–noon.

Dom St Peter

South Germany's finest Gothic cathedral was begun in 1250, after a fire destroyed an earlier one. The lace-like south and north towers, begun respectively in 1341 and 1383, point 105m (344ft) skywards and were completed only in 1869. The exterior is rich in medieval carving, especially the west doorway, which features statues of St George and St Martin, and the humorous figures known locally as 'the Devil and his Grandma'. The interior is enriched by 13th- and 14th-century stained glass. Look for the 15th-century rib-vaulted Gothic cloister and the All Saints' chapel, with mid-11th-century architectural features. If you can visit on Sunday, attend Mass to hear the 'Cathedral Sparrows', a boys' choir known worldwide.

Domplatz. Open: 9am–5.30pm. Guided tours: May–Oct, Mon–Sat 10am, 11am & 2pm, Sun noon & 2pm; Nov–Apr, Mon–Sat 11am, Sun noon. Free admission.

Goliath Haus

This 13th-century house takes its name from an exterior fresco of David

Apostles and angels guard the door to St Peter's Cathedral in Regensburg

WALHALLA

Downstream from Regensburg at Donaustauf is this extraordinary national monument, modelled on the Parthenon in Athens. The brainchild of King Ludwig I, it was built to honour the great and good of Germany's long history, whose portrait busts are displayed within. You can reach the monument by car or, better still, by boat along the Danube (though you must climb 358 steps from the pier).

Boat trips depart regularly from Regensburg from 23 March to 20 October; the journey lasts 45 minutes each way. (More details from the tourist office.)

and Goliath, painted by Melchior Bocks-berger in the 1570s.
Goliathstrasse.

Historisches Museum

A wonderfully detailed scale model of the city, along with archaeological finds and works of art by members of the Danube school of painters, including Albrecht Altdorfer.
Dachauplatz 2–4. Open: Tue–Sun 10am–4pm. Admission charge.

Porta Praetoria

The remains of this Roman gateway date from the time when the city was first founded in the reign of Marcus Aurelius in AD 179.
Unter den Schwibbögen.

St Emmeran and Schloss Thurn und Taxis

Once the chapel of a Benedictine monastery, the crypt of this church dates from the mid-8th century, and its nave was exuberantly stuccoed and decorated in the 18th century by the Asam brothers. The monastery itself was acquired in 1812 by the Princess von Thurn und Taxis (whose family became immensely rich by running Germany's postal system), and she converted it into a palace. The family continued building until 1889, but retained the magical Gothic cloister.

Emmeransplatz. Church open: Mon–Thur & Sat 10am–4.30pm, Fri 1–4.30pm, Sun noon–4.30pm.
Cloister and Schloss Thurn und Taxis open for guided tours only: summer, daily 11am, 2pm, 3pm & 4pm; weekends also at 10am; winter, weekends only 10am, 11am, 2pm & 3pm. Admission charge.

St Jacob's

Founded by Irish Benedictines, and dedicated to St James, the church has a Romanesque north porch, a crucifix of 1180 and puzzling sculptures on its façade.
Schottenstrasse. Open: 9am–5.30pm.

Steinerne Brücke

The view across Germany's oldest stone bridge (built between 1135 and 1146) is breathtaking; it takes in the city's gateways and towers, the venerable old houses with their dormer windows and the two fretted spires of the cathedral.

Regensburg is 118km (73 miles) northeast of Munich. Tourist office: Altes Rathaus, Rathausplatz 3. Tel: (0941) 507 3411; fax: (0941) 507 4419; www.regensburg.de

Regensburg, on the banks of the Danube

Rothenburg ob der Tauber

The most romantic town in Bavaria is perched above the winding River Tauber and surrounded by 2.5km (1¹/₂ miles) of medieval walls, along which you can walk. Time seems to have stood still here since the 16th century.

The focal point of the town is Marktplatz. Here you will find the arcaded Rathaus (Town Hall), half of which is 13th-century Gothic, the other half Renaissance, having been built in 1578 by Leonhard Weidemann. It has a splendid tower dating from the 16th century with views from the top. Inside the Town Hall are dungeons, a gruesome torture chamber and a Gothic-style Imperial Hall where justice was dispensed (*open: tower, daily 9.30am–12.30pm & 1–5pm; town hall: 9.30am–5.30pm*).

The Ratstrinkstube of 1446 stands to the right of the Rathaus. In the baroque gable end there is a shuttered window that opens several times a day (*at 11am, noon, 1pm, 2pm, 3pm, 9pm & 10pm*) to reveal mechanical figures that re-enact a pivotal moment during the Thirty Years' War; one figure represents the Catholic General Tilly who agreed not to sack the town if the *Bürgermeister* (Mayor) could drink three litres of wine in one draught. The *Bürgermeister* succeeded in downing the wine and for this feat the city was saved.

The tallest building in Rothenburg is the church of St Jakob, in Kirchplatz, a 14th-century basilica whose two crocketed spires rise high above the town's red-tiled roofs. It has many treasures, including 14th-century stained glass and a mid-15th-century high altar on whose panels Friedrich Herlin painted scenes from the legend of

Time stands still in Rothenburg ob der Tauber, one of Bavaria's most picturesque towns

Enjoying the outdoor life outside
Weiden's Altes Rathaus

St James the Great, incorporating into
one panel a picture of Rothenburg in
the 15th century. Above all the other
treasures, this church shelters a tour de
force by Tilman Riemenschneider, the
Holy Blood Altar, which was carved in
1505 and depicts the Last Supper (*open:
daily 9am–5.30pm; admission charge*).
*84km (52 miles) west of Nürnberg.
Tourist office: Marktplatz 2.
Tel: (09861) 404 800; fax: (09861) 404
529; www.rothenburg.de*

Straubing

Gabled houses, the 14th-century, 68-m
(223-ft) high belfry in the main square,
Stadtplatz, and a Renaissance fountain
all add charm to Straubing, so that one
can readily forget that in 1445 the local
duke had his wife, Agnes Bernauer,
drowned in the river, erroneously
suspecting her of witchcraft. In
penitence for this, he built a chapel for
her in the atmospheric cemetery of St
Peter's, the town's fine Romanesque
church. Equally splendid is Jakobskirche,
a magnificent Gothic church built of

brick and designed by Hans Stethaimer.
It has 15th-century stained glass and
frescoes, as well as baroque decoration
by the Asam brothers and an 85-m
(279-ft) high belfry. In the town
museum, you can see a rich hoard of
Roman treasures, including gold masks,
probably buried when the site, now
occupied by the town, served as a
frontier post on the Danube.
*47km (29 miles) southeast of Regensburg.
Tourist office: Theresienplatz 20.
Tel: (09421) 944 307; fax: (09421) 944
103; www.straubing.de*

Weiden

Situated in the valley of the Waldnaab,
Weiden is a sizeable place, with modern
residential and industrial quarters
surrounding an attractive old town. It
was founded in the early 13th century on
the trading route between Prague and
Nürnberg, and it greatly profited from
this strategic position during the next
two centuries. Evidence of this is the
Altes Rathaus (Old Town Hall), a gabled
building of 1539–45, with an octagonal
tower topped with a Renaissance dome.
Equally impressive is the Altes Schulhaus
(Old Schoolhouse), a seven-storey
building dating from 1566.

The two belfries of Josephskirche rise
high above the houses of Weiden, and
although it is a neo-Romanesque
building of 1900, the interior is
pleasingly decorated in the Art
Nouveau style.
*97km (60 miles) north of Regensburg.
Tourist office: in the Max-Reger-Halle.
Tel: (0961) 480 8250; fax: (0961) 480
8251; e-mail: tourist-information@
weiden-oberpfalz.de*

Tour: the Romantische Strasse

Germany's oldest, most beguiling tourist road stretches for 350km (217 miles) from Würzburg in the northwest, via Augsburg to Füssen in the south on the Austrian border. The road passes through many medieval and Renaissance villages and towns. You could take a week or more to drive the route if you stop at all the destinations described below.

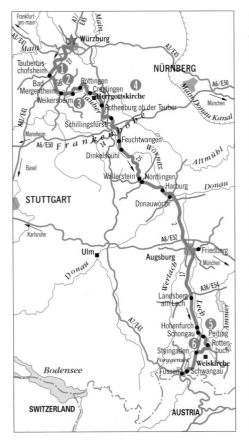

Leave Würzburg (see pp126–7 & pp130–31) by the B27 and drive southwest for 32km (20 miles) to Tauberbischofsheim.

1 Tauberbischofsheim

Set in the Tauber valley, this is an unspoiled wine village of half-timbered houses, some sculpted with mermaids. Franconian wines can be sampled every first and third Saturday of the month in the basement of the 14th-century castle, which also houses a local history museum (*open: Easter–Oct, Tue–Sun 2.30–4.30pm, Sun 10am–noon; closed: Mon*).
Drive 18km (11 miles) southeast on the B290 to Bad Mergentheim.

2 Bad Mergentheim

The more modern spa town flourishes alongside the older town where you can see the Renaissance Deutschorden-schloss, the castle of the Grand Master of the Order of Teutonic Knights (*open: Tue–Sun 10am–5pm; closed: Mon;*

www.deutschordensmuseum.de). Several Grand Masters lie buried in the crypt of the 18th-century castle church (by Balthasar Neumann and François Cuvilliés).

Green signs, with lettering in yellow, now direct you along the route. After driving east for 11km (7 miles) on the B19, you reach Weikersheim.

3 Weikersheim

The town is dominated by the moated Renaissance palace of the Hohenlohe family, who ruled the region, with its magnificent baroque garden.

Continue east through half-timbered Röttingen, shortly turning south to reach Creglingen.

4 Creglingen

Just outside the town is the Herrgottskirche, a church of 1380 housing Tilman Riemenschneider's masterpiece, the 7-m (23-ft) high Altar of Our Lady, carved out of limewood in 1505.

Drive 18km (11 miles) southeast to Rothenburg ob der Tauber (see pp108–9). The route now continues southeast with a detour through the baroque town of Schillingsfürst, then passes through medieval Feuchtwangen, Dinkelsbühl, Nördlingen and Donauwörth. The B2 takes you to Augsburg (see pp82–3). The route then continues on the B17 through Landsberg am Lech (see p88), Hohenfurch and the walled health resort of Schongau with its fjord-like lake. The Romantische Strasse then arrives at Peiting.

5 Peiting

This market town, situated between the Rivers Ammer and Lech, is a popular winter sports centre. In summer it makes a good walking base – local shops sell the hiking map (*Wanderkarte*) that details a hike along the so-called King Ludwig's Route to Rottenbuch. Alternatively, drive on to this town.

6 Rottenbuch

The interior of the church of Maria Geburt, all that remains of an Augustinian convent founded in 1074, is a rococo confection by local artists including the accomplished Matthäus Günther.

The route continues west to Steingaden, with its Romanesque monastery and the nearby pilgrimage Wieskirche. This is one of the most magnificent rococo churches in Bavaria, its perfectly composed interior décor amongst the finest achievements of the Zimmermann brothers.

Finally the Romantische Strasse curves its way southwest to Schwangau (see p92) and Füssen (see pp84–5). Also see www.romantischestrasse.de

Bad Mergentheim's Renaissance castle

Northern Bavaria

Aschaffenburg

Aschaffenburg is a town of majestic buildings and green parks situated on a bluff above the right bank of the River Main. Its Altstadt (old town), located between the huge sandstone castle and the Stiftskirche, has twisting streets, welcoming inns and half-timbered houses. It is the perfect starting point for excursions into the Spessart forest.

Schloss Johannisburg

Once the residence of the Electors and Bishops of Mainz, this huge building of red sandstone was designed by Georg Ridinger of Strasbourg and built between the 15th and 18th centuries.

Today, it serves as the city art gallery and the fine state rooms are hung with works by German and Flemish artists, most notably Lukas Cranach. Some of the original furniture dates from the late 18th century.

Open: Tue–Sun, Apr–Sept,
9am–5.30pm; Oct–Mar, 10am–4pm.
Closed: Mon.
Admission charge.

Schönbusch Park

Laid out in the 18th century, this is one of Germany's oldest formal gardens. The park is enlivened by a little castle set beside a lake, by a classical temple, pavilions, a maze and a restaurant.

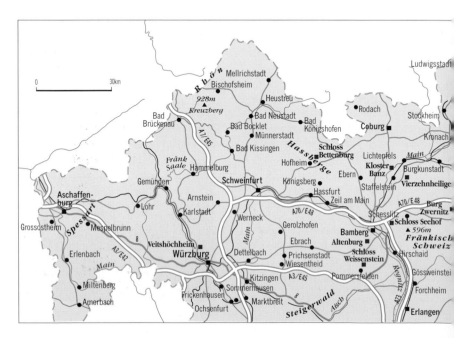

Schloss Johannisburg, Aschaffenburg, built as a palace for the Bishops of Mainz

Stiftskirche St Peter und St Alexander

The oldest church in Aschaffenburg was built in the 12th century, with a late Romanesque cloister and a 15th-century tower. It houses a 12th-century crucifix and a rare painting – *Lamentation* by Matthias Grünewald.
Dalbergstrasse. Open: Mon–Sat 9am–dusk, Sun noon–dusk.

Aschaffenburg is 70km (43 miles) northwest of Würzburg.
Tourist office: Schlossplatz 1.
Tel: (06021) 395 800;
fax: (06021) 395 802;
e-mail: tourist@info-aschaffenburg.de

Bamberg

Set, like Rome, on seven hills, the university city of Bamberg rose to prominence nearly 1,000 years ago. Heinrich II, who became Holy Roman Emperor in 1014, regarded this as his favourite city and lies buried in its cathedral. The River Regnitz divides the city into its ecclesiastical and its secular parts, though the former town hall, entrancingly straddling the river, symbolically unites them. The virtually traffic-free island on the Regnitz hosts a flea market on Untere Brücke, presided over by a statue of Heinrich II's wife, St Kunigunde. A concert hall has been especially built for the city's symphony orchestra, one of the best in Germany. Bamberg has ten breweries and four beer gardens (to which you can take your own food), while a half-hour trip down the River Main takes you to the Franconian vineyards.

Alte Hofhaltung

The former prince-bishops' residence, next to the cathedral, with its Renaissance façade and Gothic court-yard, is now the city's history museum. *Domplatz 7. Open: May–Oct, Tue–Sun 9am–5pm; open for exhibitions during winter. Closed: Mon.*

Altenburg Schloss

Situated on the highest of the city's seven hills, with its moat, battlemented walls, keep and neo-Gothic chapel, the former bishop's castle is fronted by an 18th-century Crucifixion group by Georg Adam Reuss. It now houses a restaurant, and there are splendid views over Bamberg from the terrace.

Carmelite Monastery

The late-Romanesque cloister dates from the 13th century, while the rest of the buildings are baroque, transformed by Leonhard Dientzenhofer in 1692. *Karmelitenplatz. Open: daily 9–11.30am & 2.30–5.30pm.*

Kaiserdom

The four Gothic towers of the city's great 13th-century cathedral dominate the splendid **Domplatz** (Cathedral Square). On the Princes' Portal expressive carvings depict the *Last Judgement*.

Among the cathedral's superb works of art is the *Bamberger Reiter* (Bamberg Knight), an exquisite equestrian statue sculpted around 1230. In the west chancel is the tomb of Pope Clement II (the only papal tomb north of the Alps). The sarcophagus of Emperor Heinrich (Henry) II and his wife, Kunigunde, was created in 1513 (some 450 years after their deaths) by Tilman Riemen-schneider. Another superb group of medieval carvings in the cathedral shows the Jewish Synagogue (a blindfolded woman), the Christian Church, and the Virgin Mary and her cousin Elizabeth. The south transept contains the celebrated *Marienalter* (1523) carved by Veit Stoss, with the tiny infant Jesus watched over by his mother. The cathedral museum is in the chapterhouse built by Balthasar Neumann in 1730.
Open: 9am–5.30pm. Museum open: Tue–Sun 10am–5pm.

Kleine Venedig

Stretching downstream alongside the River Regnitz from Bamberg's Rathaus

(Town Hall) is a row of fisherfolk's houses. These are part of the water-lapped and picturesque quarter known as Bamberg's Little Venice.

Neue Residenz

This huge baroque building was created for Prince-Bishop Lothar Franz von Schönborn between 1697 and 1703 by the architect Johann Dientzenhofer. Its most imposing room is the Emperor's Hall, but all the rooms are splendidly decorated. Behind the building is a beautiful Rose Garden with a view of the former Benedictine abbey of St Michael. *Open. daily, Apr–Sept 9am 6pm, Thur until 8pm; Oct–Mar 10am–4pm. Admission charge.*

St Michael

Towering above the city and once the chapel of a Benedictine monastery, the church now has a superb baroque façade and flight of steps by Leonhard Dientzenhofer. Inside, Romanesque pillars support Gothic vaults with paintings of medicinal herbs. The pulpit of 1751 was designed by Georg Adam Reuss. Other monastic buildings by Dientzenhofer and his brothers and Balthasar Neumann shelter an old people's home, two restaurants and a brewery museum.
Open: 9am–5.30pm. Brewery museum open: Thur–Sun 1–4pm. Admission charge.

Bamberg is 61km (38 miles) north of Nürnberg. Tourist office: Geyerswörthstrasse 3. Tel: (0951) 871 161; fax: (0951) 871 960; www.tourismus.bamberg.de

Bamberg's Altes Rathaus

The town that Wagner made his home

Bayreuth

Although Bayreuth today is universally associated with Wagner, its musical traditions date back to the early 15th-century rule of Margrave Friedrich I. In the 17th century his successors, the Margraves of Brandenburg-Kulmbach, made Bayreuth their principal home, enticing here Italian and Prussian, as well as Bavarian, musicians.

In the mid-18th century one of the Margraves married the cultured Princess Wilhelmina of Prussia, elder sister of Frederich the Great, who inspired the court with new artistic standards. In 1764 her husband commissioned an architect from Bologna, Giuseppe Galli-Bibiena, to build an opera house, and it was this lovely building that entranced Richard Wagner in 1871 when he was seeking a concert hall large enough to mount his Ring cycle. Franz Liszt, father of Wagner's wife, Cosima, was another composer attracted to Bayreuth; today, he lies buried in the town's cemetery.

Altes Schloss

The older of Bayreuth's two castles was begun in the 14th century but was largely rebuilt in the 1750s. Its 18th-century chapel was designed by the French architect François Joseph de Saint-Pierre. It now houses council offices. *Maximilianstrasse.*

Festspielhaus

Wagner had this Festival Hall built in 1872–6 on a hill north of the town. The pink-and-white building resembles an amphitheatre and seats 1,800 people. It hosts the annual Bayreuth Wagner Festival in late July and August.
Festspielhügel 1–2.
Tel: (0921) 78780;
www.festspiele.de.
Open: guided tours only Tue–Sun 10am, 10.45am, 2.15pm & 3pm.
Closed: Mon & Nov.

Haus Wahnfried

Richard Wagner built this villa for himself in 1873. It now serves as a museum dedicated to his life, his music and his friends, including Mathilde Wesendonck who inspired *Tristan and Isolde.* Wagner and his wife Cosima are buried in the villa grounds.
Richard Wagner Strasse 48.
www.wagnermuseum.de.
Open: daily summer

EREMITAGE

Situated 4km (2½ miles) east of Bayreuth is the 18th-century Eremitage (Hermitage), where members of the court would go to dress up as shepherds and shepherdesses and enjoy the 'simple' pleasures.

In its park is a rococo Temple of the Sun, a Hermit's Chapel, a Dragon's Den, several fountains and cascades, and the grave of Wilhelmina's pet dog, built as a ruin.
Eremitagestrasse.
Open: Apr–15 Oct daily 9am–6pm, Thur until 8pm. Closed: 16 Oct–Mar. Admission charge.

9am–5pm, till 8pm on Tue & Thur; winter 10am–5pm. Admission charge.

Markgräfliches Opernhaus

This opera house, built by Giuseppe Galli-Bibiena in the 1740s, is infinitely more seductive than the one built for Richard Wagner. Its galleried interior is a superb melange of baroque reds, golds and greens.

Opernstrasse 14. Open: Tue–Sun 9am–6pm, until 8pm on Thur; winter, daily 10am–4pm. Admission charge.

Neues Schloss

Built in the mid-1750s, the Schloss is full of finely decorated rooms and galleries, including a Japanese Room and a Hall of Mirrors. It faces a fantastical fountain designed by Elias Räntz in 1700. The pictures in the Schloss demonstrate Princess Wilhelmina's love of Asian art. Also worth a visit is the Bayreuth Faïence museum. Behind the castle is the Hofgarten which was laid out in 1609.

Ludwigstrasse 21. Open: daily, Apr–Sept 9am–6pm, until 8pm on Thur; winter 10am–4pm. Admission charge.

Bayreuth is 67km (42 miles) northeast of Nürnberg.
Tourist office: Luitpoldplatz 9.
Tel: (0921) 88588; fax: (0921) 88555; www.bayreuth-tourismus.de

Neues Schloss and the ornate fountain facing it

Wagner in Bavaria

In 1861, the future King Ludwig II of Bavaria (*see pp94–5*) heard Richard Wagner's opera *Lohengrin* and was enthralled. Almost immediately after becoming king in 1864, he promised Wagner (then in hiding from his creditors) that he would 'banish from you the petty cares of everyday life, allowing you to spread the mighty wings of your genius'. The degree to which Ludwig II idolised Wagner can be seen at Schloss Hohenschwangau (*see p92*), where Ludwig entertained his protégé and which is crammed with Wagner memorabilia (including the composer's piano and his bust set next to a gilt-framed portrait of the king), while at Neuschwanstein (*see p93*) the rooms are decorated with scenes from the composer's greatest operas.

Ludwig paid off Wagner's debts, for which the composer was enormously grateful: 'Long after

we are dead,' wrote the composer, 'our work will continue to delight and dazzle the centuries.' Wagner's next opera, *Tristan und Isolde*, was staged at Munich in 1865 and was a triumph.

Their friendship proved disastrous for

the king, however, for Wagner's revolutionary connections alarmed the monarch's advisers. They were even more concerned at the amount of money the king was spending on his friend, and in 1865 the two men were forced to part.

Ludwig had planned a Wagnerian opera house in Munich but was forced to abandon the project. Wagner set about raising his own funds to build a theatre in Bayreuth (spurning as too small the exquisite baroque Markgräfliches Opernhaus, even though

it had initially attracted him to the town). Aided by massive loans, he eventually succeeded in building the Festspielhaus (*see p116*), which opened in 1876 with the first complete performance of his three-part work, *Der Ring der Nibelungen*.

Management of the Festspielhaus has remained within the hands of the Wagner family ever since. At Wagner's death in 1883, his widow Cosima took over. She was followed by their son, Siegfred, who also composed operas. Siegfred's wife, Winifred Williams, directed the Bayreuth Festival until 1944. Wagner's grandsons, Wieland and Wolfgang, took over in 1951, and Wolfgang became the theatre's sole director after Wieland died in 1966.

Evidence of Bavaria's pride in Wagner – Facing page: Scenes from *Die Meistersinger* decorate the walls of Schloss Neuschwanstein; above: Schloss Hohenschwangau, filled with Wagnerian items

Hassfurt's Gothic church of St Kilian

Coburg
In the 19th century Coburg's dukes and duchesses had the knack of marrying well. Among their number was Prince Leopold of Saxe-Coburg, who became the first king of Belgium in 1831. One of his sisters married the Duke of Kent, and their daughter, Victoria, ascended the British throne in 1837. Queen Victoria then married Prince Albert of Saxe-Coburg. Other scions of the family succeeded to the thrones of Portugal, Belgium and Bulgaria. The town of Coburg is dominated by the splendid Veste (Fortress), which was home to this illustrious family until they moved into the Ehrenburg in the lower town.

Ehrenburg
The ducal residence from 1547 to 1918, this castle is part Renaissance and part 19th-century neo-Gothic. The splendid Hall of Giants is so-called because of the 28 figures that hold up the ceiling.
Schlossplatz. Guided tours: Tue–Sun, Apr–Sept every hour 9am–5pm; Oct–Mar every hour 10am–3pm. Admission charge.

Puppenmuseum
This appealing museum displays doll's houses, dolls and toys dating from 1810 to 1950.
Rückertstrasse 2–3. Open: Apr–Oct, daily 9am–5pm; Nov–Mar, Tue–Sun 10am–5pm.

Veste Coburg
One of Germany's largest and best-preserved medieval fortresses, Veste Coburg sits on a spur high above the town. Because of its tower-studded outline, it is often called the 'Crown of Franconia'. Dating back to the 11th century, most of the present fortress was rebuilt in the 16th and 17th centuries. In 1530, the Protestant reformer Martin Luther took refuge here, and you can see the room where he stayed.

Veste Coburg houses a massive collection of engravings, some 350,000 in total, representing every European school. You can also see displays of hunting weapons and weapons of war, carriages, furniture, glassware, porcelain and paintings from the Middle Ages to the 20th century.
Guided tours: Tue–Sun, Apr–Oct 10am–5pm; Nov–Mar 1–4pm. Closed: Mon. Admission charge.

Coburg is 100km (62 miles) north of Nürnberg. Tourist office: Herrngasse 4. Tel: (09561) 74180; fax: (09561) 741 837; www.coburg-tourist.de

Hassfurt
Still partly surrounded by its medieval fortifications, Hassfurt retains its remarkable grid of streets, laid out in chequerboard fashion in the 13th

century. Most of the town's buildings date to the 16th century. One of these is the three-storey Rathaus (Town Hall) of 1521 with its stuccoed hall and portraits of the prince-bishops who ruled the town.

The 14th-century Ritterkapelle served the nobility of Hassfurt and is copiously decorated with their coats of arms – 248 of them on a frieze and 28 others sculpted on the keystones of the arches.

Rising in the town's main square, Marktplatz, the parish church of St Kilian was founded in 1390. Sadly, the baroque interior was destroyed in the 19th century to make way for a neo-Gothic refashioning, but some lovely treasures remain inside the building; they include two masterpieces by Tilman Riemenschneider, a statue of the Virgin and another of St John the Baptist.

The hilly country surrounding Hassfurt, which lies between the Hass mountains and the Steiger woods, is crisscrossed with hiking routes and sprinkled with ruined castles.

30km (19 miles) northwest of Bamberg.
Tourist office: Hauptstrasse 5.
Tel: (09521) 688 227; fax: (09521) 688 280; e-mail: info@hassfurt.de

Hofheim

Hofheim is a town of charming half-timbered houses situated on the western side of the Hass mountains. Among these houses is the Apotheke, a pharmacy built in 1581. The parish church is a late-Gothic building that houses a sculpture of St Mary and St John (1460), as well as some fine baroque statues.

14km (9 miles) north of Hassfurt, 45km (28 miles) northwest of Bamberg.
Tourist office: Obere Sennigstrasse 4.
Tel: (09523) 92290; fax: (09523) 267.

Schloss Bettenburg
3km (2 miles) north of Hofheim, the castle has stood here since 1343 and was mostly rebuilt from 1537. In the 19th century, Christian Truchsess von Wetzhausen transformed the Schloss into a music centre.

A pleasant courtyard within the Veste Coburg fortress

Kronach

The most celebrated son of Kronach was the artist Lucas Cranach the Elder, who was born here in 1472, and went on to become the court painter to the Protestant Elector Friedrich the Wise at Wittenberg.

The most historic part of Kronach, with its medieval heart, is the picturesque upper town. Here you will find the Altes Rathaus (Old Town Hall), a Renaissance building with a 17th-century entrance, and numerous coats of arms carved in stone. There are guided tours available on request.

Above the town rises the mighty **Festung Rosenberg**, a 12th-century medieval fortress with a triple ring of walls and only one entrance. It was redesigned by Balthasar Neumann in the 1730s as a refuge for the Bishops of Bamberg, to which city Kronach belonged for 700 years. Part of it is now a youth hostel, while its south wing houses the **Frankische Galerie**, a branch of the Bavarian National Gallery, devoted to Franconian art from the Middle Ages to the Renaissance. On show are sculptural masterpieces by Tilman Riemenschneider, Veit Stoss and Adam Krafft.

45km (28 miles) northwest of Bayreuth.
Tourist office: Marktplatz 5.
Tel: (09261) 97236;
e-mail: ti-kronach@gmx.de.
Frankische Galerie open: Apr–Oct 9am–6pm, Nov–Mar 10am–4pm.
Closed: Mon. Admission charge.

Kulmbach

This quaint old town has a famous brewery producing Kulmbacher Eisbock – said to be the strongest beer in the world. It is overlooked by the **Veste Plassenburg**, the finest Renaissance fortress in Franconia. The mid 12th-century castle was rebuilt mainly by Caspar Vischer in the 1560s. Today it houses several museums, including the **Zinnfigurenmuseum**, a national collection of some 300,000 tin figurines.

23km (14 miles) northwest of Bayreuth.
Tourist office: Sutte 2.
Tel: (09221) 95880; fax: (09221) 958 844;
e-mail: touristinfo@stadt-kulmbach.de.
Zinnfigurenmuseum open: daily, Apr–Oct 10am–5pm, until 8pm on Thur;
Nov–Mar 10am–4pm. Admission charge.

Ochsenfurt

Literally translated, Ochsenfurt means 'ox ford', though today you do not have to wade across the River Main – it is spanned by the Mainbrücke, a bridge built of wood in the 13th century and later replaced in stone. The town retains its well-preserved 14th-century fortifications and many picturesque half-timbered houses, especially along Hauptstrasse and Brückenstrasse. Its emblem is the clock tower in the town hall whose mannequins have performed for the citizens since 1560.

The clock figures merely enhance the most entrancing late-Gothic town hall in Franconia. Construction of the Rathaus began at the start of the 16th century, and the eight-sided clock tower (topped with a spire) was added in 1560. Dormer windows and an open-air staircase with elaborate balustrades all add to the ambience, while the Councillors' Hall has a painted Renaissance ceiling. Another important building is the impressive 13th-century church of St Andreas which still retains its tower of 1288, though the chapels were not finished until the late 15th century and the chapel dedicated to St Johann Nepomuk dates from the 18th century. The spacious Renaissance high altar of 1612 is the masterpiece of a relatively unknown sculptor, Georg Brenck, who was born in Windsheim. The church's octagonal bronze font was created in the 1720s. The finest sculpture here is that of St Nicholas by Tilman Riemenschneider.

20km (12 miles) south of Würzburg.
Tourist office: Hauptstrasse 39.
Tel: (09331) 5855;
fax: (09331) 7493.

Ochsenfurt's pretty main street leads to the splendid Rathaus

Pommersfelden

Pommersfelden is famous as the location of Schloss Weissenstein, one of Bavaria's most sumptuous palaces. The Schloss was built between 1711 and 1718 by Johann Dientzenhofer for Prince-Bishop Lothar-Franz von Schönborn, who held many positions and titles, including those of arch-chancellor of the Holy Roman Empire, Bishop of Bamberg and Archbishop-Elector of Mainz. Later on, his palace was further enhanced by the skills of the Mainz architect Maximilian von Welsch and the Viennese architect Johann Lukas von Hildebrandt, court architect to the Habsburgs.

The central building, with its imposing entrance hall, is flanked by two wings and looks on to a

The central pavilion of Schloss Weissenstein in Pommersfelden formal garden and courtyard (the Ehrenhof) as well as the crescent-shaped mews which Maximilian von Welsch added in 1714. The supreme glory of this palace is its staircase. Prince-Bishop Lothar-Franz himself dabbled in architecture and, with the help of von Hildebrandt, designed this staircase himself. The double flight of stairs rises to the first floor, which is surmounted by two galleries overlooking a huge well. In 1718, JR Byss decorated its ceiling with a *trompe l'oeil* depiction of the four corners of the world, surveyed by the ancient Greek gods of Olympus.

Other treats are the Grotto Hall, lit by chandeliers and decorated with stucco sea shells and leaves, a pink dining room, a Hall of Mirrors, and the marble hall, which rises to the height of five storeys. This last displays portraits of the Schönborn family as well as idealised depictions of Italian artists. The Banqueting Hall is still laid out for ghostly 18th-century personages to sit and eat. Dispersed throughout the Schloss are paintings by such masters as Rembrandt, Peter Paul Rubens, Titian, Albrecht Dürer and Peter Brueghel. Schloss Weissenstein also has a restaurant, and hosts concerts from July to mid-August.

26km (16 miles) south of Bamberg. Tours: Apr–Oct, daily 10am–5pm. Admission charge.

Vierzehnheiligen

In the mid-15th century, 14 saints (*Vierzehnheiligen* in German), along with the Infant Jesus, repeatedly revealed themselves to a devout shepherd named Hermann Leicht who lived beside the River Main just south of Lichtenfels. He inspired the abbot of nearby Banz to build a little pilgrimage chapel high on the left bank of the river, on the spot where they had appeared.

Two centuries later this chapel was attracting so many pilgrims that Balthasar Neumann was commissioned to build a new church big enough to accommodate them all. Along with his pupils and the Italian fresco master Appiani, Neumann created what can only be called the most outrageously flamboyant baroque church in Germany, though the rather plain and conventional exterior gives no clues to the fanciful decoration within. Your sensibilities are likely to whirl once you step inside this sensuous building. Everything is a delightful froth of well-lit stucco decoration painted pink, white and gold. The focal point is JM Küchel's altar, depicting the 14 saints, which goes over the top in dazzling wildness, though Appiani's ceiling frescoes well match this exuberance. Nothing here is placid, everything is overwrought, yet the whole is coherently brilliant.

Between Staffelstein and Lichtenfels, 30km (19 miles) northeast of Bamberg. Open: 9am–5.30pm.

Kloster Banz

On a plateau rising on the opposite side of the River Main to Vierzehnheiligen is the monastery of Banz. Founded in 1069, the monastery was ruined in the Thirty Years' War and rebuilt by Johann Leonhard Dientzenhofer, assisted by his brothers and by Balthasar Neumann. The monastery chapel is superbly frescoed and contains sumptuous furnishings. There are also splendid views from the church terrace over the Main Valley to Vierzehnheiligen.

Würzburg

The history of this ancient university town stretches back to 1000 BC, when Celts first built a hill fort on the heights now occupied by the Marienberg fortress. Würzburg derives its name from the Castellum Virteburg founded by the Franks in the mid-7th century. Irish missionaries, led by St Kilian, were martyred here in 689, having failed to convert the inhabitants to Christianity, but the town was the seat of a bishop from 742, and in 1168 Frederick Barbarossa elevated them to the status of prince-bishops. The university was founded in 1582, and after the Thirty Years' War the prince-bishop of the day fortified the city and began building the superb Residenz.

This, and other fine buildings, earned Würzburg the title 'Jewel of the Main'. Disaster struck the city, however, in March 1945 when an air raid left the centre almost entirely destroyed. Würzburg today is a university and

Würzburg's Residenz, built for the town's powerful prince-bishops

business city that cherishes its ancient heart and preserves numerous celebrated inns serving the local Franconian wine. The city straddles both banks of the River Main, the two halves linked by the ornate Alte Mainbrücke (the Old Main Bridge). Most of the sights of the old town on the west bank are described in the walk on page 130. In addition, there are the following sights dotted around the edges of the city.

Festung Marienberg

Festung Marienberg began life as a hill fort around 1000 BC, and from then on the hill always had some kind of fortification on its summit. The present fortress has Renaissance and baroque elements, and the armoury of 1712 now houses the superb **Mainfränkisches Museum**, whose works of art include masterpieces by Tilman Riemenschneider (*see pp128–9*). In the Princes' Wing (the Fürstenbau), an exhibition recounts the history of Würzburg over the last 1,200 years.

Museums open: Apr–Oct, Tue–Sun 10am–5pm. The Mainfränkisches Museum is closed on Mon and closes at 4pm in winter. The Fürstenbaumuseum is closed Nov–Mar. Admission charge.

Käppele

This pilgrimage church on the west bank of the Main escaped bombing during World War II because of its relatively isolated position. It was built by Balthasar Neumann in 1748 and has a sumptuous interior with stucco work by Joseph Anton Feuchtmayr and frescoes by Matthäus Günther.

Würzburg (*see walk on pp130–31 for route*)

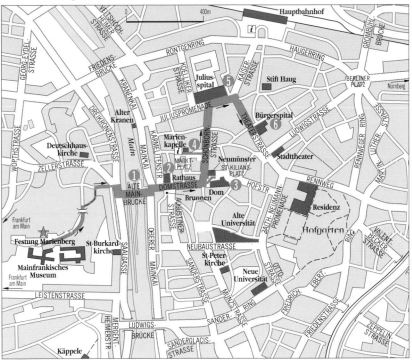

Residenz

Designed by Balthasar Neumann, this palace of the prince-bishops of Würzburg constitutes one of southern Germany's greatest baroque buildings. It was built between 1720 and 1744 with the help of Maximilian von Welsch and the Viennese architect Lukas von Hildebrandt. The triumphal staircase rises beneath a cantilevered dome that is painted with a huge ceiling fresco by the Venetian artist Giovanni Battista Tiepolo. The Emperor's Hall also has frescoes by Tiepolo, and he was responsible for the altar paintings of the lavish court chapel. The gardens are filled with statues and have magnificent rococo wrought-iron gates (*see p134*).

Open: daily, Apr–mid-Oct 9am–6pm, until 8pm on Thur; winter 10am–4pm. Admission charge.

Stift Haug

Built between 1670 and 1691, this was the first baroque church to be built in Franconia, and its architect was the Italian Petrini. Over the main altar is a Crucifixion painted in 1683 by the Venetian painter Tintoretto.

Würzburg is 103km (64 miles) northwest of Nürnberg.
Tourist office: Am Congress Centrum. Tel: (0931) 372 335; fax: (0931) 373 652; www.wuerzburg.de/tourismus

Bavarian carving

Bavaria's greatest sculptor, Tilman Riemenschneider (1460–1531), came to Würzburg in 1483 and eventually rose to become *bürgermeister* (Mayor) of the town. Many of his limewood, marble and sandstone masterpieces are displayed in the Mainfränkisches Museum in Festung Marienberg (*see p126*). They include his sandstone figures of Adam and Eve, which are among the most tenderly humane works of the late medieval period.

Another of his superb sculptures, representing the Virgin and St John weeping over the dead body of Christ, is to be found in Würzburg's Martin-von-Wagner Museum. For the parish church of Hessenthal in the Spessart, he carved another quite different, equally exquisite *Lamentation*. Other masterpieces include the tomb of St Heinrich and St Kunigunde in Bamberg Cathedral (*see p114*) and his entrancing carving of the Madonna in the pilgrimage church at Volkach.

Perhaps his greatest work is the *Holy Blood Altar* (so-called because it

houses a crystal containing what is claimed to be a drop of Christ's own blood) carved between 1501 and 1505 for the church of St Jakob, Rothenburg ob der Tauber (*see p108*). In this work, which depicts the *Last Supper*, Jesus and his disciples are individually characterised, while the wings of the altarpiece dramatically represent Jesus's triumphant entry into Jerusalem on Palm Sunday and his anguish on the Mount of Olives.

Riemenschneider stands in a long tradition of Bavarian carving, as can be seen from the statues in Bamberg Cathedral (*see p114*). His contemporary, Veit Stoss, sculpted a sublime *Annunciation* which can be seen in Nürnberg Cathedral (*see p105*), while another contemporary, Erasmus Grasser, created the delightful set of folk dancers now displayed in Munich's Stadtmuseum (*see p50*). Two decades later the brilliant Hans Leinberger was working in Landshut (*see pp68–9*), where he carved the *Landshut Madonna* and a superb tomb for the church of St Martin.

Bavaria's baroque master carvers matched the accomplishments of their medieval predecessors. Even minor artists, such as Ignaz Weibel who carved the prior's stall (1691) for the Klosterkirche at Buxheim, produced masterpieces. And the Bavarian woodcarving tradition lives on, particularly at Oberammergau.

Right: tomb carving in Bamberg's cathedral; facing page and above: the carving tradition continues in modern Oberammergau with superb examples found in many of the country's museums

Walk: Würzburg

This walk takes you through the lively heart of old Würzburg. *See page 127 for a map of the route.* *Allow 1 hour.*

Start at Festung Marienberg (see p126). From April to November, bus 9 (Festungsbus) will save you the uphill climb. After enjoying a panoramic view of the old city, walk from the Marienberg down to the Alte Mainbrücke.

1 Alte Mainbrücke

Built between 1473 and 1543, the Alte Mainbrücke spans the River Main and is adorned with numerous statues of saints added in the 18th century. They include the Virgin Mary (patron saint of Franconia), the infant Jesus and St Joseph, St John Nepomuk (patron saint of bridges, since he was martyred by drowning), St Burkard the first Bishop of Würzburg, and King Pepin and his son Charlemagne, the first Holy Roman Emperor.

To the north of the bridge, beside the river, you will spot an ancient crane (Alte Kranen), once used for unloading trading ships, which dates to around 1770, close to which is the House of Franconian Wines.

As you walk up Domstrasse from the bridge, you will see a baroque fountain created in 1765 by L von der Auvera and Peter Wagner, elaborately sculpted with figures representing the four Cardinal Virtues and topped by a statue of the Virgin.

2 Rathaus

The town hall rises beside its fountain. It has a 55-m (180-ft) high late Renaissance tower, and the Wenceslas Hall (named after the king of Bohemia) dates to the 13th century. The Roter Bau (Red Building), a late Renaissance building of 1659 with a baroque façade, adjoins the Rathaus. Today the city council meets in the south wing of the town hall, while the Ratskeller serves food and drink in the open central courtyard. Guided tours are offered May to October every Saturday at 10am.
Follow Domstrasse up to St-Kilians-Platz, site of one of Germany's largest Romanesque cathedrals.

3 The Dom and the Neumünster

The cathedral of St Kilian, begun in 1040, is dedicated to the Irish missionary who arrived here in AD 686. It was later enriched by a 15th-century Gothic cloister and by the chapel of the Prince-Bishops of Würzburg. Inside are sculptural masterpieces by Tilman Riemenschneider (especially a carving of Rudolf von Scherenberg). Just north of the cathedral stands the Neumünster, built over the grave of St Kilian, with its curving baroque façade and its sweeping staircase. Founded in the 12th century, the church was totally rebuilt in the early 18th century by Johann Dientzenhofer.

Walk north along Schönbornstrasse and turn left into the city's main square, Marktplatz.

4 Marienkapelle

This Gothic building that dominates Marktplatz is decorated with statues of Adam and Eve, copies of Riemenschneider's original, now in the Mainfränkisches Museum (*see p126*).

Near the entrance is the tomb of Balthasar Neumann, the city's greatest architect, and there are several fine medieval knights' tombstones within.

Return to Schönbornstrasse, turn left, and walk to Juliusspital at the end.

5 Juliusspital

This imposing almshouse was founded in 1576 by Prince-Bishop Julius Echter and reconstructed after a fire of 1699 by the Italian baroque architect Antonio Petrini. It incorporates a rococo pharmacy, with sculptures by Johann Peter Wagner, and a baroque fountain of 1706 symbolising Franconia's four rivers and designed by Jakob van der Auvera. In the atmospheric cellars, you can buy wine by the glass, by the carafe or by the bottle.

Turn right along Juliuspromenade, and second right into Theaterstrasse to find the Bürgerspital, halfway down on the left.

6 Bürgerspital

An even older charitable institution than the Juliusspital, the Bürgerspital was founded by rich citizens in 1316 to care for the town's aged and needy. It still does and, like the Juliusspital, derives its income chiefly from selling the wines of its extensive vineyards. The Bürgerspital is also blessed with a Gothic church, housing precious carvings, and an arcaded early 18th-century courtyard.
www.buergerspital.de

The panoramic view of the old city from the Festung Marienberg

Getting away from it all

PARKS AND GARDENS

Bavaria abounds in superb parks, often set around palaces, many of them dating from the period following the Thirty Years' War (1618–48) when the region's gardeners were influenced by the French baroque style (and above all by the gardens of Louis XIV's palace of Versailles). Towards the end of the 18th century, gardens became less formal and far more picturesque; this was the period when the so-called 'English' style was developed, particularly by Friedrich Ludwig von Sckell.

Ansbach

The **Hofgarten** was laid out as a baroque garden in the first half of the 18th century and landscaped in the 1780s. The 18th-century orangery is fronted by colourful flowerbeds. *See p98.*
Open: daily sunrise–sunset.
Free admission.

Spring colours in the borders of Ansbach's delightful Hofgarten

Aschaffenburg

Beside the River Main, 3km (2 miles) west of the town, is Schönbusch (*see p112*), a park laid out in 1778 around a Schloss belonging to the Archbishop of Mainz. It was designed by Joseph Emanuel d'Herigoyen and later landscaped by Friedrich Ludwig von Sckell. Scattered throughout the park in pleasing contrast with the other classical buildings are picturesque follies, such as shepherds' huts and Dutch-style cottages.
Open: daily. Free admission.

Bayreuth

Bayreuth boasts two superb gardens. The first surrounds Schloss Eremitage (*see p116*), so-called because the castle was built to resemble a monastery, or hermitage, in 1715. A second castle in the same garden was completed in 1753. Grottoes, water-jets and fake ruins (such as a 'Roman' theatre) dot the park, which was laid out from 1736 and later landscaped in the English fashion.
4km (2¹/₂ miles) northeast of Bayreuth.
Open: daily. Fountains play May–Oct, 9am–5pm on the hour. Free admission.

The second garden, called **Sanspareil**, was laid out in the mid-18th century as a 'wild' park, with beech trees, rock formations, and rustic buildings. On a hill above the garden is Burg Zwernitz, a castle which can also be visited.
On the A505 between Bayreuth and Bamberg. Buildings in park and Burg Zwernitz open: Apr–Sept, Tue–Sun 9am–6pm. Admission charge. Gardens open: daily. Free admission.

Linderhof

Laid out by Karl Effner in the 1880s to surround one of King Ludwig II's castles (*see pp88–9*), these gardens reveal the king's passion for all things French. The ornamental flower beds take the shape of Bourbon lilies, while the western and eastern parterres have busts of Louis XIV and Louis XVI respectively. Cascades flow down the steeply terraced slopes. The 'Venus Grotto' has an underground lake and tableaux simulating the first act of Wagner's opera *Tannhäuser*. Ludwig also bought a Moorish kiosk from a Berlin railway magnate and erected it in the garden.
20km (12 miles) southwest of Oberammergau.
Open: summer, daily 9am–5.30pm (Thur until 8pm);

winter 10am–4pm.
Gardens: Free admission.

München

The city has numerous parks and gardens, including the **Englischer Garten** (*see pp36–7*), and the Alter Botanischer Garten near the station.

Schloss Nymphenburg

As initially laid out by its two French gardeners, the baroque style of the park surrounding Schloss Nymphenburg

A non-floral exhibit in Munich's Alter Botanischer Garten

(*see pp58–9*), with its lovely pools, deliberately mimicked the garden of Versailles without slavishly copying it. When it was redesigned by Friedrich Ludwig von Sckell at the start of the 19th century, he did not discard the original baroque design but integrated it with the new with remarkable success.
Open: daily, May–Aug 6am–9.30pm, Other times until sunset; winter 6am–5pm. Free admission to the gardens.

Botanical Garden
Set beside Schloss Nymphenburg is a botanical garden, laid out in 1914 for the Bavarian Science Academy. Here you can study at close quarters specimens of the plants that grow in the region, including Alpine plants, rhododendrons, heathers and ferns.
www.botanik.biologie.uni-muenchen.de. Open: daily, May–Aug 9am–7pm, until 5pm in winter. Admission charge.

Schloss Schleissheim
The attractive baroque garden of Neues Schloss Schleissheim is the work of Dominique Girard, a French designer who had worked at Versailles. It has a splendid cascade that falls to a sunken parterre.
Open: daily. Free admission.

Weihenstephan
This former monastery garden is located just south of Freising, next to the Weihenstephan Brewery on a hill called Weihenstephaner Berg. It displays some 800 varieties of rose and 250 types of peony as well as numerous perennials, shrubs and ornamental trees.
Open: daily. Free admission.

Würzburg
Hofgarten
Balthasar Neumann conceived the notion of integrating the long façade of the Residenz with the old fortifications of Würzburg by means of a lavish garden embodying subtly created terraces (*see p127*). In 1774 Johann Prokop Mayer, court gardener to Prince-Bishop Adam Friedrich von Seinsheim, began work on the eastern section of this sumptuous garden. He created the terraces, joined together either by flights of steps or by ramps. Sculptures and balustrades add to the glamour, as do arbours of larch and laburnum.

Mayer next turned his attention to the south garden. Terminating in an orangery, this garden was later landscaped in the English style, informally incorporating lawns and trees. Some of the latter are magnificent, including clipped pyramids of 200-year-old yew trees, as well as cypresses, magnolias, limes and plane trees, and an avenue of oriental ginkgoes.
Open: daily 7am–sunset. Free admission.

Schloss Veitshöchheim
The baroque palace in this village, 7km (4 miles) north of the city, was built by the prince-bishops of Würzburg as their summer residence. Here, in the 1760s, Prince-Bishop Adam Friedrich von Seinsheim commissioned Johann Prokop Mayer to design what eventually became Germany's finest surviving rococo garden. He was able to utilise the Grosser See, a large formal lake already created by 1703, as well as some baroque elements of the earlier garden that Balthasar Neumann had designed.

A grid of hedges and walks, arbours and Chinese pavilions, and statuary by Peter Wagner and Ferdinand Tietz complete an exquisite ensemble of 18th-century garden design.

Schloss open: Apr–Oct, Tue–Sun 9am–noon & 1–5pm. Admission charge. Garden open: 7am–sunset. Free admission.

LAKES AND RIVERS

In Oberbayern (Upper Bavaria) the waters of over 20 lakes ripple amid superb mountain and tree-clad scenery. Watersports are allowed on most of the lakes, though such activities are banned on some in order to preserve the plant and animal life along their shores. Sports flourish particularly on the Ammersee, the Chiemsee (*see pp66–7*), the Starnberger See, the Schliersee and the Tegernsee. Some Bavarian lakes are

exceedingly cold because of their depth, while others, such as the Auwaldsee, the Riegsee, the Schliersee, the Staffelsee and the Wörthsee, are warm enough to make sport and swimming a pleasant activity in summer.

Starnberger See

The region around the Starnberg Lake is dubbed the Fünf-Seen-Land ('Five Lakes Land') and its lakeside towns are readily reached from Munich using the S-Bahn 5 or 6 trains. A typically attractive resort catering for these lakes is the fishing village of Münsing, situated on a ridge between the Isar and the Starnberger See. Here a 13-km (8-mile) stretch of the lake's shore is reserved for holidaymakers, with activities ranging from surfing to steamship excursions. *www.5seenlandinfo.de*

Lindau's pretty lakeside harbour on the Bodensee (Lake Constance)

Bodensee

At the extreme southwest of Bavaria, Lindau borders the Bodensee (Lake Constance), where you can swim, windsurf, water-ski and fish. This is a curiously mild region, with orchards and outdoor cafés by the lakeside. You can also take a boat trip to the island of Mainau, which has been transformed into a floral park full of orchids, tulips, dahlias, lilies, roses and rhododendrons.

East Allgäu

Further east are the four major lakes of the East Allgäu, all of them visible from Schloss Neuschwanstein: the Forggensee, the Schwansee, the Hopfsee and the Bannwaldsee. The region is in fact washed by a number of lakes, 30 in all, whose shore length totals an amazing 115km (71 miles).

Bad Tölz

Five per cent of the Bad Tölz region consists of lakes, amongst the most popular being the Tegernsee, the Walchensee, the Bibisee (near Königsdorf) and the Kirchsee (close to Sachsenkam).

Enchanting towns and villages guard the shores of these lakes. A visit to Kochel am See, beside the Walchensee, offers a chance of fishing, sailing, rowing, surfing and swimming.

Danube tours

A cruise along the Danube offers relief from hectic sightseeing. Passau is an excellent starting point, and you can choose from a variety of tours, including an 8-day return trip to Budapest, or a 4-day return trip to Vienna.

In summer, Regensburg is a centre for shorter cruises along the Danube, for example to Walhalla or Mariaort. Kelheim is a third centre, from which you can sail as far as Regensburg through a deep gorge, some of the river's most spectacular reaches. *Cruises from Passau are arranged by the DER Reisebüro, in the Nibelungenhalle, Dr Hans-Kapfinger-Strasse 7 (tel: (0851) 71017) or Wurm & Köck, Höllgasse 26 (tel: (0851) 929 292). For cruises from Regensburg contact Personenschifffahrt Klinger, Werftstrasse 8 (tel: (0941) 55359). Kelheim has several cruise companies, among them MDK-Schifffahrt Altmühltal, Schlossweg 3 (tel: (09441) 207 125) and Personenschifffahrt Schweiger, Rennweg 32 (tel: (09441) 3402). The latter also depart from Regensburg.*

NATIONAL PARKS

Bavaria rejoices in several nature and national parks which are managed in such a way as to leave the ecosystems as undisturbed as possible while granting access to serious visitors. Given below are some of Bavaria's finest protected areas.

Altmühl Valley Nature Park

Rare plants, birds and butterflies inhabit the juniper- and grass-covered heathlands of the Altmühl Valley. Fossil-hunters are encouraged, and you can borrow geological hammers in the quarries of Eichstätt-Blumenberg and Mörnsheim-Apfeltal.

Once completely covered by the sea, the valley is rich in fossils and skeletons dating back to 150 million years ago. It was in this area that the fossil skeletons of the oldest known bird,

Archaeopteryx, were found and are preserved in the Bürgermeister-Müller-Museum at Solnhofen and in the Jura-Museum at Eichstätt (*see p100*).
The Altmühl Nature Park information office is housed in a former monastery at Eichstätt. Tel: (08421) 98760; e-mail: umweltzentrum@naturpark-altmuehltal.de

Augsburg's Westliche Wälder Nature Park

This is Swabia's sole nature park, covering 115,500ha (285,396 acres) and bordered by the Rivers Danube, Lech and Mindel. The terrain is hilly and comprises tree-shaded slopes rising up from gentle meadows watered by softly flowing streams. Around 40 per cent of the park is under forest cover that shelters animals and plants, some of them rare.

Since 1984, the Westliche Wälder Nature Park information office has been accommodated in the baroque Oberschönenfeld Cistercian monastery at Gessertshausen (*open: daily, except Mon, 10am–5pm; tel: (08238) 31010; geschaeftsstelle@naturpark-augsburg.de*), where you can obtain information on the climate, woods and meadowland, soil and colonisation, and also the flora and fauna of the park. Also at the monastery is a beer garden and the Swabian Folklore Museum.

Befreiungshalle (Liberation Monument) commemorating Napoleon's defeat overlooks the Altmühl Valley at Kelheim

Limestone mountains, beech woods and Alpine meadows at Berchtesgaden

Bavarian Forest National Park

The Nationalpark Bayerischer Wald is Germany's oldest national park (1970). Parts of it adjoin the National Park Bohemian Forest (in the Czech Republic) to form the largest (1,000sq km/386sq miles) cross-border national park in central Europe. It also adjoins the even larger, but less strictly protected, Naturpark Bayerischer Wald, which encompasses an area of some 3,000sq km (1,158sq miles). The highest peak in the national park is the 1,453-m (4,767-ft) high Rachel; however, the highest peak in the Bavarian Forest region is the 1,456-m (4,777-ft) Grosser Arber, to the northwest in the Naturpark.

Just outside the national park, the glass-blowing villages of Spiegelau, Frauenau and Zwiesel add allure to the region, as do lonely pilgrimage churches and stern fortresses. Hotels, guesthouses and private rooms welcome visitors, many of whom come in winter to enjoy cross-country skiing. To enable naturalists to study the exceptional flora and fauna of this region, there are 200km (124 miles) of marked walks within the national park, as well as geological zones set aside for those interested in studying the rock formations.

For further information, contact the Informationszentrum Hans-Eisenmann-Haus, 94556 Neuschönau. Tel: (08558) 96150; www.nationalpark-bayerischer-wald.de

Berchtesgaden National Park

Bordering the Austrian province of Salzburg, this park, established in 1978, covers some 210sq km (81sq miles). Ancient limestone mountains surround its exquisite lake. Deciduous forests (mostly of beech) cover almost half the park and are a spectacular sight in autumn when their leaves turn to gold. The beech forest grades into conifers, such as spruce and pine, at higher elevations. These forests rise as high as 800m (2,625ft), while at 1,800m (5,906ft) and above, rare Alpine vegetation scrapes a living among the rock debris and crevices. Alpine meadows alternate with areas of alder and dwarf pine. Lakes and rivers wash the region.

Open to visitors throughout the year, the park has 230km (143 miles) of marked paths and climbing routes. It also has several mountain huts with catering facilities.

Berchtesgaden National Park information offices: Franziskanerplatz 7, Berchtesgaden (tel: (08652) 64343); & the former railway station at Schönau am Königssee (tel: (08652) 62222).

Verdant countryside of the Bavarian Alpenstrasse

Shopping

Huge department stores mix with elegant boutiques and useful everyday supermarkets in the shopping area between Marienplatz and Karlsplatz (also known as Stachus) in Munich. Munich is also an international fashion centre, and if you want expensive clothing, you should head for the elegant shops along Maximilianstrasse and Theatinerstrasse.

Pick up a souvenir made from natural materials

Both men and women will be attracted to **Loden-Frey** in Maffeistrasse, the premier Munich outlet for traditional Bavarian costumes, such as Loden-coats made out of long-lasting, thick, weatherproof green cloth, matched by feathered hats. Diagonally opposite the shop is the rococo-fronted **Wallach-Haus**, its name deriving from Moritz Wallach who began producing the city's famous hand-printed materials in 1900; its store is crammed with these lovely fabrics as well as attractive souvenir tablecloths.

Parts of Munich resemble one huge antique market, particularly the area round Barerstrasse and Briennerstrasse, while cheaper bargains are to be found in Türkenstrasse in Schwabing (to the west of the Englischer Garten). Schwabing remains a student area, and its characterful offbeat shops, between Münchener Freiheit and the Siegestor, proclaim that 'the unusual is always in fashion'.

Beyond the capital

One of Augsburg's most charming innovations has been the transformation of the narrow streets and medieval houses of the Untere Stadt into a shopping area full of antique shops and boutiques, while two other pedestrianised zones house a number of modern shops.

Aschaffenburg is another Bavarian town that has made its main shopping centre into a pedestrianised precinct, and at Regensburg the ambience of the Altstadt, the upper town, is enhanced by a multitude of small shops, many of them selling antiques; larger department stores are in the more modern part of the city.

A noted centre for antiques, Bamberg boasts many dealers specialising in baroque art (try those in Karolinenstrasse). The city has also revived its tradition of fine weaving. There is a noted flea market on the island in the middle of the River Regnitz between the two parts of the city.

Nürnberg has numerous fashionable boutiques and department stores, and it attracts bargain-hunters to its Trempelmarkt, a flea market that sells antiquities, bric-a-brac and art. Jewellery, glass and porcelain are also good buys here. It takes place twice a year, in May and September.

Kaufingerstrasse is a popular spot for shopping

At Würzburg you should buy Franconian wine. The best sources in town for this are the **Bürgerspital** on the corner of Theaterstrasse and Semmelstrasse; the **House of** **Franconian Wines** at Kranenkai 1; the **Hofkeller** in the Rosenbachpalais on Residenzplatz; and the **Weineck Julius Echter** (the outlet of the Juliusspital) at Koellikerstrasse 1–2.

Munich's central market offers a bewildering range of items from which to choose

MARKETS

Undoubtedly, the most celebrated market in Bavaria is Munich's Viktualienmarkt (*see pp52–3*). With its maypole and its stalls covered with gaily coloured awnings, this has been Munich's central market since 1807. The market's three fountains are decorated with statues of Munich's best-loved humorists and singers: Karl Valentin (1882–1948), Weiss Ferdl (1882–1949) and Liesl Karlstadt (1892–1960). Its booths and shops sell local vegetables, flowers, fish, fruit, herbs, cheese and drink, as well as goods from many other countries. Hearty, inexpensive but delicious food, washed down by beer, is sold in little taverns half-open to the elements, as well as in the Viktualienmarkt's beer garden.

The plethora of Bavaria's local markets is displayed at Regensburg, whose general market (*on Kumpfmühler Strasse; Wednesdays and Saturdays, closing at noon*) is supplemented by a Monday and Saturday flower market on Altdorferplatz, a daily fruit and vegetable market in the Alter Kornmarkt, and a potato market on weekdays in Wöhrdstrasse and Werftstrasse. Almost every city enjoys a similar number and variety of markets.

Christmas markets

Every city and town worth its salt hosts a *Christkindlmarkt*, following a tradition begun in Nürnberg in the mid-16th century. From the Friday before Advent until Christmas Eve, Nürnberg's streets are festooned with garlands and lights. Children's choirs and brass bands perform beside the city's stupendous fountain. Surrounding a Christmas crib in the centre of the Hauptmarkt, fir-clad stalls sell Christmas decorations, decorated candles, local handicrafts, and little figures made of dried fruit and crêpe paper called *Zwetschgenmännle* ('plum people'). Other stalls offer Nürnberg's little pork sausages and the honey and gingerbread cakes known as *Lebkuchen*, which visitors have with mulled red wine.

Munich's *Christkindlmarkt* lasts from the end of November to Christmas Eve and developed out of the medieval celebration of the feast of the patron saint of children, St Nikolaus (Santa Claus), which falls on 6 December. Later, the stallholders of its Viktualienmarkt cashed in on the festival and started to host a long-running Christmas fair.

Since 1972, Munich's *Christkindlmarkt* has centred on the Marienplatz and the pedestrianised zone surrounding this

A colourful maypole sets off the Viktualienmarkt

from a surfeit of angels. In 1493, Hans Holbein the Elder painted some angel musicians for the city's cathedral high altar. Today, modern Mädchen, winged like these angels, their long tresses curled, play lutes for the spectators at the *Christkindlmarkt*. Even Augsburg's *Lebkuchen* (Christmas cookies) are baked in the shape of angels.

Among the many other Bavarian Christmas markets, that at Rothenburg ob der Tauber is especially fine, in part simply because of the beauty of the setting. The stalls, selling candles, gingerbread cakes and every conceivable Christmas decoration, are set up in the Marktplatz, shaded by the arcaded town hall. On the Friday before Advent, the Bürgermeister (Mayor) and a brass band concert inaugurate the market, after which festivities continue until 20 December. Every day either a brass band or a group of singers performs in the Marktplatz. The slender, late 14th-century basilica of St Jakob hosts concerts, as well as a special *Christkindlmarkt* service, with enrapturing music, on the feast of St Nikolaus.

The ancient Bavarian craft of woodcarving is often pursued at home

square. An enormous Christmas tree decked with lights dominates the square with its maze of stalls. The air is fragrant with the scent of mulled wine and toasted almonds. From late November, Advent carols are sung here, and in the week before Christmas, you can enjoy Christmas carols in the monastery church of St Anna.

At Augsburg, visitors to the *Christkindlmarkt* are likely to suffer

CRAFTS

Bavarians are a conservative folk, and though not averse to change, they are nevertheless keen to preserve the old traditions and crafts that help make them distinctive from their fellow Germans. Traditional handicrafts flourish above all in the popular tourist region of Upper Bavaria (Oberbayern), in the rural villages of the Bavarian Forest, and in the forested regions of the Fichtelgebirge and Frankenwald, to the east and north of Bayreuth respectively.

The small town of Diessen, on the shores of the Ammersee, has a centuries-old tradition of producing fine pottery and faïence. Local potters and ceramic artists from around the world display their work at the annual *Töpfermarkt* (Potters' Market), which starts on Ascension Day and lasts four days. The work of other craftspeople, for instance pewter-making, can also be seen and bought. For a list of workshops offering courses, or which are open to visitors, inquire at the Verkehrsamt (*Mühlstrasse 4a; tel: (08807) 1048; e-mail: verkehrsamt-diessen@t-online.de*).

Oberammergau specialises in carvings of Christmas crib figures, crucifixes, and statues of the Virgin and various saints. Here, too, you can see workshops specialising in the crafts of painting on glass and modelling in wax.

The craft of glass-blowing has, for centuries, been a speciality of several

Brightly coloured straw ornaments at a Munich street market

Shoppers outside a Munich fashion store

centres in the Bavarian Forest. You can see demonstrations in Frauenau (on the edge of the Bavarian Forest National Park) at the Freiherr von Poschinger Glashütte (*Moosauhütte 12; tel: (09926) 94010; www.poschinger.de*). Mittenwald, in Oberbayern, dubs itself the Village of a Thousand Violins, a tradition deriving from 1683 when a local farmer's son, Mathias Klotz, returned home after many years working in Cremona with the celebrated violin-maker Nicolo Amati and handed down his skills to others in the town. Today, the violas and cellos of Mittenwald are exported worldwide. Few, perhaps, can afford a violin as a souvenir, but the same region, especially around Berchtesgaden, also

specialises in affordable hand-painted boxes, known as *Spanschachteln*, as well as wooden dolls and figurines.

Kulmbach (*see p122*) not only has a museum devoted to tin figures, but also hosts a tin-figure exchange market each August. By contrast, Bayreuth's favourite metal is pewter, its symbol the Bayreuther Eichala, a hand-crafted tankard with an acorn on its lid.

At Nürnberg, the half-timbered boutiques and workshops lining the narrow streets of the Handwerkerhof (Artisans' Courtyard) offer high-quality wares of traditional craftsmanship: ceramics for the house and garden; glassware; the creations of goldsmiths, silversmiths and tinsmiths; purses, belts and other leather goods; engravings; toys and dolls; and elaborate candles. Nürnberg is famed for its traditional wooden toys.

Since so much of Germany's porcelain tableware is produced in the area around Fichtelgebirge in Franconia, the region has set up a Porcelain Route (the Porzellanstrasse) through the major manufacturing centres. Information can be obtained from the tourist office (*Gablonzer Strasse 11, 95686 Fichtelberg;* *tel: (09272) 97032; e-mail: Information-Fichtelberg@Fichtelgebirge.de*).

Finally, delightful kitsch is displayed in the world-famous Maria Innocentia Hummel figures. Made by W Goebel Porzellanfabrik (*Coburger Strasse 7, 96472 Rödental, northeast of Coburg; tel: (09563) 920; www.goebel.de*), these immensely popular and wonderful porcelain recreations of children of yesteryear were designed by a Franciscan nun who was born in Bavaria in 1909.

Woodcarved souvenirs for sale in Bavaria

Folk dances in Bavaria are far subtler than the traditional image of people slapping their clogs and each other's cheeks (sometimes promulgated in a tongue-in-cheek fashion by the Bavarians themselves). These dances are characteristic only of Bavaria's southernmost regions. Other regions have preserved their own rich dance traditions. In Lower Bavaria at fairs and festivals you come across more than 100 different dances. The Upper Palatinate specialises in

Zweifachen, a dance with changes in rhythm, whereas in Upper Franconia, open-air folk dancing (especially at the fairs) culminates in Bavaria's fastest dance, which is rightly dubbed 'The Gallop'.

Dialect songs are still popular in Upper Bavaria, where regional Christmas carols are especially prized. Traditional musical instruments – the zither and the alpenhorn, for instance – add charm to Bavarian folk evenings.

Bavarians so relish their national costumes that throughout the Free State, hundreds of national costume clubs have been formed. Each region of Bavaria has its own distinctive costume, the result of their origins. In Franconia, for example, the national dress dates back, in the main, to the 18th century, so when the citizens bring out their finest garb for festivals and

fairs, the scene is distinctly baroque. In the Alpine regions, by contrast, traditional costumes for the most part have developed out of hunting clothes. Upper Bavarians can be recognised by their leather shorts, their feathered hats and their woollen jackets.

Centuries-old traditions remain

Many aspects of Bavarian folklore are part of a living tradition enjoyed (and sometimes satirised) by every generation

unchanged in parts of Bavaria. One example is the feast of St Michael the Archangel, known as Michaeli, celebrated in the Bavarian Alps on 29 September. This is the date on which cowherds traditionally bring their animals down to the safety of the valleys before the advent of the winter snow. Dressed in traditional costumes, they also deck the heads of their beasts with crowns created from flowers and sprays of spruce and larch.

Entertainment

Bavaria offers a wide variety of top-class entertainment, ranging from classical ballet to pop and jazz. This is true not only of Munich, but of all the major cities, and even tiny villages. The list that follows covers only the major centres and inevitably omits some entrancing spectacles, but local tourist offices amply supply the visitor with details of what is happening.

Prinzregententheater

MUNICH

The city mounts an opera festival from June to the beginning of August. Summer concerts frequently take place in the city's fine palaces, particularly Schloss Nymphenburg, Schloss Blutenburg and the castle at Dachau.

Around the 22nd of each month the Munich tourist office publishes an inexpensive official monthly programme (*Monatsprogramm*) which can be obtained in the tourist office, at newspaper stands and in many book shops. This lists theatre, music and exhibition schedules.

Classical music and theatre

Classical and modern plays are performed in the **Residenztheater** and in the **Kammerspiele im Schauspielhaus** (*Maximilianstrasse 26*).

The **Bavarian State Opera House** (the Nationaltheater on Max-Joseph-Platz) hosts ballet and occasional concerts as well as opera.

Smaller operas are also staged in the **Cuvilliés-Theater**. The **Gasteig-Kulturzentrum** (Gasteig Cultural Centre) boasts a fine new concert hall. Light opera, operetta, musicals and ballet are performed in the **Staatstheater am Gärtnerplatz**.

Free concerts

Students of the Richard Strauss Conservatory play free of charge in the Kleine Konzertsaal of the **Gasteig Cultural Centre** on weekdays from 6.15pm. Also free are many of the concerts given by the **Music Academy** at Arcisstrasse 12.

Specialist theatres

Munich's youth theatre (Schauburg) is located at Franz-Joseph-Strasse 47. For avant-garde theatre, visit the **Marstalltheater** and **Werkraumtheater**.

Rock and pop

The favourite venues for rock and pop concerts include the **Olympic Hall**, the **Colosseum** and the **Circus Krone**. For good rock music during the week, try the **Wirthaus im Schlachthof** at Zenettistrasse 9.

Tickets

For opera and other performances at the Nationaltheater, the advance sales office is at Max-Joseph-Platz 2 (*open: Mon–*

Fri 10am–6pm, Sat 10am–1pm; closed on Sun). In the evenings tickets can be bought at the same office an hour before each performance. There are reductions for students, subject to the availability of tickets. You can also buy cheaper tickets provided that you are willing to stand and watch.

The box office at the Staatstheater am Gärtnerplatz (open: Mon–Fri 10am–6pm, Sat 10am–1pm; closed on Sun) offers cheap tickets for standing room. The Staatstheater box office opens an hour before performances. Tickets at the Staatstheater can also be booked online at: www.staatstheater-am-gaertnerplatz.de

The Olympic Hall box office is at the Ice Stadium, Olympic Park (open: Mon–Fri 10am–6pm, Sat 10am–3pm; tel: (089) 5481 8181).

Buy tickets for the Cuvilliés-Theater at Max-Joseph-Platz 2, and for the Gasteig Cultural Centre at Rosenheimer Strasse 5 (tel: (089) 5481 8181; open: Mon–Fri 10am–8pm, Sat 10am–4pm; closed on Sun).

Tickets for concerts, and many other events, can also be booked through München Ticket, in the Rathaus on Marienplatz (the office is open Mon–Fri 10am–8pm, Sat 10am–4pm; tel: (089) 5481 8181; for internet bookings: e-mail: info@muenchenticket.de; www.muenchenticket.de).

The imposing exterior of the Munich Opera House

Augsburg

Proud of its Mozart connections, Augsburg occasionally offers concerts in the house where the composer's father, Leopold, was born, along with readings from Wolfgang's letters to his cousin. In the same house is the headquarters of the German Mozart Society, which is dedicated to promoting and organising festivals of the composer's works.

Of course Mozart's is not the only classical music that can be heard in the city. The Augsburg Cathedral Boys' Choir, the Kammersolisten (Chamber Soloists) and the Madrigal Choir offer a combined repertoire ranging from baroque to modern classical music. A real treat is the chance to hear chamber music performed in the mid-eighteenth-century Kleiner Goldener Saal (*Jesuitengasse 12*).

Theater Augsburg's Grosses Haus, on Kennedyplatz 1, stages opera, ballet and drama, while the Kongresshalle (Congress Hall) is the venue for symphony concerts (*Gögginger Strasse 10*). The Kömodie hosts plays and ballet and has a studio for plays and chamber music (*Vorderer Lech 8*). The Freilichtbühne stages opera and operetta (*Am Roten Tor 5*). All theatre

Coburg's Landestheater

booking offices open for ticket sales one hour before performances begin. To book in advance for any of these theatres call at the vestibule of the Theater Augsburg on weekdays 9am–6.30pm and Saturdays 10am–4pm (*tel: (0821) 324 4900*). Tickets can also be booked at the Augsburg tourist office. They also publish a useful annual preview (*Veranstaltungskalender*) of each year's happenings.

Bamberg

In June and July, the municipal theatre leaves its usual home, the ETA Hoffmann Theater on Schillerplatz, to mount the open-air Calderón Festival in the courtyard of the Alte Hofhaltung (the former Residenz beside the cathedral). The theatre also has a studio at Markusplatz 12 (*for advance bookings, tel: (0951) 871 433*).

Bamberg also has its own symphony orchestra and a youth orchestra, both of which perform in the city's Konzert-und Kongresshalle, Mussstrasse 1. Organ concerts are regularly given in the cathedral. Further information is available from the tourist office (*Geyers-wörthstrasse 3; tel: (0951) 871 161*).

Bayreuth

Trumpet fanfares announce the opening of the festival that Richard Wagner founded at Bayreuth in 1876. Undoubtedly, this remains the most prestigious annual musical event in Bavaria. The festival runs from late July to the end of August, but tickets need to be ordered the previous September (at the very latest) from the Bayreuther Festspiele, *Kartenbüro, Postfach 100262, D-95402 Bayreuth*. Only postal applications are accepted. Even then, your chances of getting a seat are low, as demand is high and the waiting list is always long.

Tickets that have been returned are sold at the Kartenbüro 10am–noon on the day of a performance, and also 1½ hours before it begins. Queues have often already formed by 6am! However, the Bayreuth cultural scene does not slacken for the rest of the year – it has a full programme of musical events including, for example, a spring festival (24–28 May) known as the Fränkische Festwoche.

Coburg

Coburg's Landestheater am Schlossplatz (formerly the Court Theatre) seats 500 and is host to varied productions, including jazz, ballet and opera (*box office tel: (09561) 92742*). Opposite stands the Studio Theatre (the Reithalle), which mounts modern drama.

From 17 to 21 May Coburg mounts the annual Coburger Convent festival, dominated by student fencing fraternities. There is also a funfair, the Vogelschiessen, in the week before the beginning of the annual school summer holidays (usually mid-July), when competitors vie for the title 'King of Marksmen', a tradition deriving from the foundation of the Coburg Marksmen's Club in 1354.

The tourist office (*Herrngasse 4; tel: (09561) 74180*) publishes a monthly calendar of events, listing the forthcoming happenings in the town.

Lindau

The Stadttheater in Barfüsserplatz is notable for being a former convent church. Here the Bodensee Symphony Orchestra performs, alternating with chamber music ensembles and a selection of international plays – the emphasis being on 20th-century dramatists such as George Bernard Shaw, Bertolt Brecht, Jean Anouilh and Arthur Miller.

For information about performances and local events, ring the tourist office (*tel: (08382) 260 030*).

Nürnberg (Nuremberg)

Theater Nürnberg, at Richard-Wagner-Platz 2–10, offers concerts, ballet, opera and drama in its spacious auditoriums (*for information about performances tel: (0911) 231 4000; for advance booking, tel: (0180) 134 4276*). Experimental theatre is mounted in the new Tafelhalle (*Äussere Sulzbacher Strasse 62; tel: (0911) 231 4000 for advance bookings*).

The Meistersingerhalle (*Münchener Strasse 21; tel: (0911) 231 8000; www.meistersingerhalle.nuernberg.de*) mounts pop and jazz as well as classical concerts. Other venues for jazz, rock or folk include the Jazz Studio (*Paniersplatz 2729; tel: (0911) 224 384*) and the Schmelztiegel (*Bergstrasse 21; tel: (0911) 244 9859*).

The sounds of jazz, rock and traditional music mix with the screams from the roller-coaster rides at the annual *Frühlingsfest* (Spring Festival), which lasts two weeks, beginning on Easter Saturday. Every even year, the city hosts a major jazz festival in June, while classical, jazz and folk concerts take place in July and August in the ruins of the church of St Katharina. Around Whitsun, major rock bands gather in Nürnberg's Frankenstadion for the 'Rock in the Park' festival, and in July or August (dates vary, consult the tourist office) musicians meet for the Bardentreffen in the Altstadt (Old Town). Finally, Nürnberg is renowned for its international organ week, which lasts from the last week in June to the first week in July.

Passau

Since 1952, Passau has been staging the 'European Weeks' every summer – a blend of opera, operetta, music, ballet, pantomime, concerts, drama, public readings by distinguished writers, and exhibitions. For information and tickets, apply to the Kartenzentrale der Europäischen Wochen Passau, Nibelungenhalle, 94032 Passau (*tel: (0851) 752 020; www.ew-passau.de*).

The city's theatre in Gottfried-Schäffer-Strasse was once the prince-bishops' opera house (*for advance bookings, tel: (0851) 929 1913*). Passau's Scharfrichter Haus at Milchgasse 2 is a popular venue for cabaret and jazz music (*tel: (0851) 35900*).

Regensburg

Regensburg's municipal theatre, where you can enjoy opera, operetta, plays and concerts, is at Bismarckplatz 7 (*box office tel: (0941) 507 2424*). In summer, the city offers open-air performances in the courtyard of the Thon-Dittmer-Palais (inquire at the tourist office) and mounts drama, cabaret, musicals and light entertainment in the Turm-Theater of the Goliath House (*Watmarkt 5; tel: (0941) 562 233*). Regensburg's folk theatre (*Stadtamhof 5; tel: (0941) 85958*) is only for those who can understand plays in the local dialect. For cabaret try the Statt-Theater (*Winklergasse 16; tel: (0941) 53302; advance bookings at the tourist office, tel: (0941) 507 4410*).

Jazz buffs come to Regensburg for the annual Bavarian jazz weekend, staged at the end of July and attracting jazz bands from all over Bavaria.

Würzburg

Every year, at the end of May, Würzburg's Residenz hosts a festival of baroque music; tickets for concerts include dinner accompanied by Franconian wines – book in advance by writing to the Fränkischer Weinbauverband, *Kranenkai, 97070 Würzburg*. The city also presents an internationally renowned Mozart festival every year during the second and third weeks of June. Tickets for performances inside the Residenz itself are prized and extremely hard to come by, but music lovers have a reasonable chance of securing seats for the evening Nachtmusik concerts performed in the Residenz gardens and elsewhere during the festival period.

Moreover, Würzburg sponsors a Bach week at the end of November in the church of St Johannis – for tickets apply to the Tourist Information Office, *Falkenhaus am Markt (tel: (0931) 372 398*).

The Mainfrankentheater (*Theaterstrasse 21; tel: (0931) 390 8124*) presents drama, ballet and opera, while lighter entertainment is on hand at the Theater Chambinzky (*Valentin-Becker-Strasse 2; tel: (0931) 51262*).

You may find a zither player in your favourite beer hall!

Pilgrimages

Altötting is Bavaria's major pilgrimage centre, drawing thousands of visitors each year from all parts of the world as well as Germany. They come to pray before a statue of the Virgin Mary and the Infant Jesus, carved out of lime wood around 1300 and now housed in the town's Gnadenkapelle. Because smoke from innumerable candles has blackened the statue, they call her the Black Madonna of Altötting.

The statue has a long history of working miracles. The first occurred in 1489 when a three-year-old child drowned in the River Inn; laid upon the altar in front of this Madonna, the toddler awoke from death. Some 2,000 *ex voto* paintings (thanking the Black Madonna for her intervention) hang in and outside the chapel.

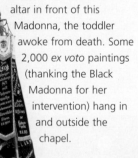

Every day her chapel is crowded with pilgrims, but the biggest gatherings take place on Sunday evenings in summer – and, above all, on the Feast of the Assumption (15 August), when crowds of pilgrims gather in the huge neo-baroque church (built in 1910) before processing with lighted candles around Altötting's massive square to pray before the Black Madonna.

Hundreds of other churches in Bavaria pull pilgrims who come to view the statues and see the relics of celebrated saints.

In Murnau, the beautiful baroque church of St Nikolas is still the goal of pilgrims. A wall of unusual *ex voto* paintings shows scenes of accidents that took place in the town and provide a record of what the central town once looked like.

One of the oldest is the monastery of Benediktbeuern, founded in 789 after the Holy Roman Emperor Charlemagne had donated a relic of St Benedict. Pilgrimages have brought prosperity to those churches fortunate enough to be endowed with a precious relic, so that sumptuous baroque buildings now shelter what were once humble and unpretentious shrines. The greatest of these is the splendid pilgrimage church of Vierzehnheiligen (*see p125*), which began as a tiny chapel and is now one of the most powerful baroque edifices in Germany.

Facing page: the church of St Nikolas (above) and a pilgrimage in traditional costume (below)
This page: abandoned crutches at Altötting (above) and little girls in traditional costume at the St Leonhard festival in Bad Tölz (below)

Children

The pleasures offered to children in Bavaria are virtually endless. In Munich, for example, the Bavaria Filmstadt (*see p32*), the Deutsches Museum (*see p34*), the Englischer Garten (*see pp36–7*), the Stadtmuseum (*see p50*) and the zoo in the Tierpark Hellabrunn (*see p61*) all appeal to young visitors. For entertainment, there is the Marionettentheater (Munich Marionette Theatre), based on a puppet theatre founded by 'Papa Schmid' in 1857.

Children in traditional costume

Located at Blumenstrasse 32 (*tel: (089) 265 712*), the current programme of the Marionettentheater is also listed in the monthly calendar of events, available from the tourist office (*U-Bahn 1, 2, 3 & 6 to Sendlinger Tor*).

The Circus Krone (*Zirkus-Krone-Strasse 1-6*) has been based in Munich since 1919 and performs from 25 December to 31 March on weekdays at 8pm (from 7 Jan it is closed on Mon); on Wednesday, Friday and Saturday also at 3pm; and on Sundays and holidays at 2.30pm and 6.30pm (*tel: (089) 558 166; www.circus-krone.de; S-Bahn to Hackerbrücke*).

Children's swings are to be found in Munich's Alte Botanischer Garten (Old Botanical Garden) and on the Theresienwiese, and there are grassy play areas set aside in the Englischer Garten (English Garden) that serve to testify the Bavarians' pleasure in entertaining their youngsters.

Such treats are repeated throughout the whole of Bavaria. Augsburg, for example, has a Marionette Theatre, offering programmes for both children and adults (*Spitalgasse 15; tel: (0821) 434 440*).

Toys and dolls are the speciality of numerous museums throughout the region, one of the finest being the **Puppenmuseum** at Coburg, with its astonishing range of lifelike dolls (*see p120*). Equally popular is the

Puppet shows are very popular with children

The vibrant festive appeal of a funfair

Weitramsdorf Schloss Tambach deer park (10km/6 miles west of Coburg), with its 200 different wildlife species, and children's playground (*tel: (09567) 922 915; open: 8am–6pm; admission charge*).

To the northeast, in nearby Neustadt bei Coburg, the **Old Christmas Factory and Christmas Museum** (Alte Weihnachtsfabrik und Weihnachtsmuseum) displays exquisitely made glass Christmas decorations, and offers demonstrations of glassblowing (*tel: (01805) 966 337; open: Tue–Sun 10am–5pm; admission charge*). Another treat is

the balloon museum at Gersthofen (near Augsburg), which styles itself the world's ballooning centre (*autobahn exit Augsburg–West; open: Sat, Sun & holidays 10am–6pm; admission charge*).

Finally, to remind youngsters of the occasional grimness of real life, take them to the school museum in Nuremberg. It is housed in the **Museum of Industrial Culture** (*Äussere Sulzbacher Strasse 62; tel: (0911) 231 3875; open: daily except Mon 10am–5pm; admission charge*). One of its interesting exhibits is a historical classroom from 1910.

Sport and leisure

The varied climate of Bavaria, its lakes, rivers and natural parks, and its Alpine region have enabled the Bavarians to develop a vast range of sporting activities. All levels of skill are catered for, from the most inexperienced to Olympic-standard champions.

Golfing at Chiemsee

The Alpine regions

Fischen and its surrounding villages, located in the southernmost part of Germany near the Allgäu Alps and set beside the River Iller, are ideally placed for those who wish to swim (in its heated pool), to cycle, hike or ride, or to play mini-golf in summer, while in winter there is skiing to enjoy or curling to watch – an ancient game similar to ice hockey that is virtually one of Bavaria's national sports (information from the Kurverwaltung, *Am Anger 15, 87538 Fischen im Allgäu; tel: (08326) 36460; fax: (08326) 364 656; www.fischen.de*).

Oberstdorf, further south, has an international figure-skating rink and 200km (124 miles) of summer footpaths (140km/87 miles in winter), as well as tennis courts, golf courses and paragliding facilities. Here you can take climbing courses and guided mountain tours (information at the Kurverwaltung, *Marktplatz 7, 87561 Oberstdorf; tel: (08322) 7000; fax: (08322) 700 236; www.oberstdorf.de; e-mail: info@oberstdorf.de*).

Further east, the Werdenfelser Land includes such famous Alpine resorts as Garmisch-Partenkirchen (*see p86*) and Oberammergau (*see p89*), as well as Mittenwald on the Upper Isar, with its 80km (50 miles) of hiking paths, its swimming, tennis and squash facilities, and, in season, rock climbing and skiing (information from the Kurverwaltung, *Dammkarstrasse 3, 82481 Mittenwald; tel: (08823) 33981; fax: (08823) 2701; www.mittenwald.de*). To the northeast of Mittenwald, you will find the resort of Bad Tölz (*see pp64–5*), while to the southwest is the Blomberg summer toboggan run.

The **Waldensee** is a mecca for windsurfers, with other watersports centres on the Kochelsee, the Isar and the Loisach. Southwest of the town of Lenggries is the Brauneck hiking country. Rising from 700m (2,297ft) to 1,700m (5,577ft), the **Brauneck** ensures snow for cross-country skiing courses and downhill ski-runs from December till Easter. The region has over 500km (311 miles) of signposted footpaths. Some 500 towns lie within this region, offering almost every type of sporting activity, including gliding at Königsdorf (information from the Verkehrsamt, *Rathausplatz 1, 83661 Lenggries; tel: (08042) 500 820; fax: (08042) 500 840; www.lenggries.de*).

Further east is the **Chiemsee** (*see p66*), with its sailing and windsurfing schools and its golf links, as well as raft trips on the River Alz. The lake and its surroundings are devoted to winter and summer sports, including winter walking tours, mountain hikes along 310km (193 miles) of signposted routes, and tennis courts. The area includes the ski resort of Aschau and the Kampenwand peak, to which visitors often go after skiing to sunbathe in the snow, taking the cable railway to the summit (information from tourist office, *see p67*).

The Berchtesgaden region (*see p66*), on the border with Austria, forms the easternmost part of Bavaria's Alpine stretch. In summer, you will find 240km (149 miles) of footpaths here, and the area is also popular for hang-gliding and kayaking; in winter, tobogganing and cross-country and Alpine skiing are the attraction. Bad Reichenhall, a little further north, has a cable car carrying climbers up to the craggy Predigtstuhl, where there is a hotel (*tel: (08651) 96850; www.predigtstuhl-hotel.de*) and excellent hiking in both summer and winter.

Hiking along the well-marked trails of the Berchtesgaden area

Sporting facilities throughout Bavaria can satisfy the most energetic as well as those who like a more leisurely approach to keeping fit. At Augsburg, for example, the tourist office provides details of cycling tours in the Naturpark Augsburg-Westliche Wälder; the city also has an 18-hole golf course, set amidst woods and lakes, to cater for this increasingly favoured sport.

The city also boasts over 200 sports clubs and gymnasiums, as well as swimming pools, ice-skating rinks, and outdoor and indoor tennis courts. For the 1972 Munich Olympics, Augsburg built the first artificial canoe slalom stadium in the world.

In Franconia, Bayreuth offers a sports centre in the middle of the town, the magnificent Kreuzstein open-air swimming pool near the university, two indoor swimming pools, an airfield open to amateur pilots and gliders, tennis courts, riding schools and a mini-golf course.

Similarly, Lindau, not content simply to offer visitors the sporting facilities of the Bodensee (Lake Constance), has numerous hotels and restaurants offering indoor bowling (for addresses of Kegelbahnen inquire at the tourist office, *see p88*), a tennis club in Am Giebelbach, two international 18-hole golf courses, five lakeside swimming pools, an ice-skating rink (which also incorporates a curling centre) and a horse-riding school.

Such facilities are available in towns and cities throughout the free state, and the following are merely an indication of the vast range of sporting facilities on offer.

The Fichtelgebirge

The most exciting part of Franconia for sporting holidays is probably this granite mountain range, located in the northeastern part of the region between Bayreuth and the frontier with the Czech Republic. There are several delightful places here that would make an ideal base. One of them is **Bischofsgrün**, a glass-making town, which lies at the foot of the highest peaks of this range (the 1,053-m/ 3,455-ft high Schneeberg, the 1,023-m/ 3,356-ft high Ochsenkopf and the 868-m/2,848-ft high Rudolfstein). Another is hill-sheltered **Bad Berneck**, at the start of the Fichtelgebirgstrasse (the scenic B303 that runs along the valley of the Weisser Main). A third is the picturesque town of Wunsiedel (3km/2 miles north of the remarkable rock formation of Luisenburg, which was created by volcanic activity some 240 million years ago).

Virtually every kind of sporting activity is promoted here: fishing, riding, tennis, squash, golf, swimming, windsurfing on the Weissenstädter Lake, flying, indoor ice-skating and parachuting. There are 400km (249 miles) of cross-country ski trails and 3,000km (1,864 miles) of marked paths (information from the tourist office at at Fichtelberg, *see p147*).

Eastern Bavaria

Regensburg is one of the main starting points for hiring boats to sail the Danube (enquire Kanu-Verleih Platzeck, *Embacher Strasse 10, 93083 Niedertraubling; tel: (09401) 51295; www.kanu-outdoor.de*). The city also has an ice stadium, thermal baths, and tennis and squash courts, while bicycles can be hired from the BikeHaus (*Hauptbahnhof, Bahnhofstrasse 18, 93047 Regensburg; tel: (0941) 599 8194*). For further addresses, contact the tourist office (*see p107*).

Upper Bavaria

Quite apart from the Bavarian Alps, Upper Bavaria offers sports freaks impeccable facilities. The Altmühl Valley Nature Park, for example, is a paradise for anglers. You can also hire a bicycle to follow some of the 500km (311 miles) of signposted tracks. Canoes and kayaks can be used along the river and on the Rhein-Main-Donau Canal, beneath the gliders that soar soundlessly over the Jura plateau (information from the tourist office in Eichstätt, *see p100*).

Kayaking the Danube at Weltenberg

Food and drink

Bavarians like to eat amply and well; indeed, 'eating and drinking hold body and soul together' is an old saying often heard in the restaurants and pubs of Munich. This part of Germany holds pleasant surprises in store for food gourmets as well as those who enjoy the simple pleasures of 'homestyle' Bavarian cooking and a frothy brew.

Austrian fare is a speciality here

Breakfast, taken between 7am and 10am, can be a complex meal, with a choice of any (or all) of boiled egg, yoghurt, fruit juice, cheeses, and various slices of ham or cooked meat extensively laid out in many hotels on a groaning table and accompanied by either tea or coffee.

Lunch, taken between noon and 2pm, can be an even ampler affair, with soup followed by a meatloaf or a leg of roast veal, served with potatoes or rice, usually accompanied by a salad, and often followed by a rich dessert cake.

If they are going to eat out in the evening, most Bavarians do so relatively early in the evening, usually between 6pm and 9pm.

Restaurants range from the characterful and inexpensive to the gourmet temples of culinary perfection with prices to match. Most restaurants display menus and prices on the wall outside or in the window. Service is included in the menu price, though a small tip is welcomed by the waiters, and the more expensive the establishment the larger the tip expected.

Some restaurants may close briefly over Christmas or New Year, especially outside the main centres or popular tourist areas.

Beer gardens serve hearty Bavarian dishes such as sausages or roast pork, and most allow you to take your own food. In unpretentious cafés all over the region you can eat similarly earthy food at keen prices – a quarter of a chicken, some *pommes frites* (chips) and a large beer will cost you less than €10.

In most restaurants there is no need to order a full menu. It is widely accepted for patrons to order just a main course and to go without dessert, should they want to do so. Nor do you necessarily have to eat local cuisine. Bavaria's many Italian restaurants serve excellent inexpensive pizzas.

While beer is certainly the beverage of choice all over Bavaria, you can also get some very good Bavarian wines, produced in Franconia, as well as wines from the Rhine and Mosel valleys of western Germany.

BAVARIAN FOOD

In Bavaria the sausage is king – whether it is the little sausages of Nürnberg, the white ones of Munich, or the magnificent 31-cm (12-inch) long Coburg sausage (its length derived from the staff carried by the statue of St Mauritius on the gable of the Rathaus). These days, however, the king must look to his laurels. At Nürnberg, the local sausages have to compete with crisply roasted shoulders of pork (*Schäuferle*). In the lakeside restaurants, fish is often a preferred delicacy. And everywhere you can find dumplings: little liver dumplings floating in meat broth, potato dumplings (*Knödel*) blended with breadcrumbs (particularly favoured in Franconia), or dumplings with wild mushrooms (*Pfifferlinge mit Semmelknödel*).

In truth, Bavaria boasts not one but many cuisines. In the Allgäu you can buy pastries known as *Nonnenfürzle* (literally 'nuns' farts'). On menus here you find pasta described as *Allgäuer Knöpfle* and served with grated mountain cheese. Often Allgäu restaurants also serve pasta (*Spätzle*) with fried onions, or with pieces of bacon and sauerkraut.

Franconia's forests provide its restaurants with wild boar, while its rivers breed fresh trout and carp, not to speak of pike, barbel, eel and perch. Potatoes help to swell the stomach throughout eastern Bavaria (where they are known as *Erdäpfel* or *Erdbirn*). Pheasant and deer that roam the forests end up cooked on eastern Bavarian tables. For pudding, the locals relish a sweet dough, fried in fat, and appearing on menus as *Ausgezogene*.

Along with its reputation for good, hearty Bavarian foods, Munich is also becoming better known for a sophisticated 'world cuisine' based on locally grown ingredients from the rich

Turn the other way if you're on a diet!

Bavarian farmlands. Look for special seasonal menus based on a favourite harvest – asparagus in May, for example. The line between Bavarian and Austrian/Hungarian cuisine has always been a blurred one, with Wiener Schnitzel and goulasch as common as any Bavarian dish.

Seasonal as well as regional varieties add complexity to Bavarian gastronomy. *Nürnberger Hutzelbrot*, for instance, is a fruit bread originating in Nürnberg and eaten during the Christmas season. Made from pears, prunes, chopped figs, chopped dates, raisins, sultanas and chopped almonds, as well as plain flour, vanilla, sugar, and a liqueur or brandy, often served buttered, it turns out to be surprisingly light.

Such a mix of ingredients in no way alarms Bavarian palates, which are used to imaginative culinary combinations. Venison and other game dishes are often served with preserved pears, blueberries or plums. *Reiberdatschi* means grated potatoes, mixed with eggs and finely chopped onions and then shaped into little cakes that are cooked in hot oil until they are brown and then served with apple sauce.

Purely vegetarian restaurants in Bavaria are still very much in the minority, but even small town restaurants serving Bavarian fare will often offer a few vegetarian dishes. Ask for *Gerichte ohne Fleisch* or simply *Gemüsegerichte* (vegetable dishes). Imaginative combinations are onions mixed with cheese and *Obatzda*, which is a tasty blend of Camembert cheese, onions, paprika, raw egg yolks and beer! Such dishes are rich, but for non-

Sausages, the base of many Bavarian meals

vegetarians there are always the richer ones. Perhaps to provide energy for the following day's skiing, you can dine heartily in the Alpine regions on a meal of braised veal topped with cream (*Kalbsrahmbraten*), finishing with baked apple dumplings (*Apfelknödel*) and marinated plums.

Throughout Bavaria, boiled beef served with horseradish is a common dish, or you can choose the juicy meat loaf known as *Leberkäs* (which literally means 'liver cheese' but in fact contains neither). A particular Munich mid-morning snack is *Weisswurst*, a fine-textured and delicately-flavoured white sausage only served before 11am.

The *Stammtisch* or host's table, which no one but the owner (host) may occupy, is a tradition of the region (*see p177*).

The following star ratings indicate the approximate cost in euros of a two-course meal, excluding beer or wine:

★	€8–16
★★	€16–25
★★★	€25 upwards

BAVARIAN FOOD IN MUNICH

Andechser am Dom ★
If you cannot make it to the monastery brewery, then this is the next best thing. Not a tourist trap.
Weinstrasse 7a.
Tel: (089) 298 481.
Open: daily 10am–1am.

Augustiner ★
A huge traditional Bavarian inn, with a beer garden, at the heart of the Innenstadt; its façade dates back to 1897.
Neuhauser Strasse 25–27.
Tel: (089) 2318 3257.
Open: daily 9am–midnight.

Blaues Haus ★
Good Bavarian and international dishes.
Hildegardstrasse 1.
Tel: (089) 2333 6977.
Open: 11am–1am.

Bogenhauser Hof ★★★
Quality Bavarian food.
Ismaningerstrasse 85.
Tel: (089) 985 586.
Open: Mon–Sat 11.30am–3pm & 6pm–1am.

Halali ★★
Specialising in game; also offering interesting fish dishes.
Schönfeldstrasse 22.
Tel: (089) 285 909.
Open: Mon–Sat noon–3pm, 6pm–1am.
Closed: Sun & holidays.

Kafer ★★★
Ask most Munich natives for the city's best restaurant and they will send you here to sample fresh local ingredients cooked traditionally, but with great flair.
Prinzregentenstrasse 73.
Tel: (089) 4168 247. Open: Mon–Sat 11am–11pm.

Königshof ★★★
Great atmosphere, great service and an outstanding wine list.
Karlspatz 25.
Tel: (089) 551 360.
Open: daily noon–3pm & 6.45–11.30pm.

Pfistermuhle ★★
The historic restaurant occupies a mill built in 1573, but the menu is an updated take on the best of Bavarian traditional dishes, with French and international accents.
Pfisterstrasse 4.

Tel: (089) 2370 3800.
Open: Mon–Sat 11.30am–11pm.

Weisses Bräuhaus ★
About as rustic as they come in Munich. Don't forget your *Lederhosen!*
Tal 7. Tel: (089) 299 875.
Open: 7am–midnight.

Wirtshaus zum Straubinger ★★
Rustic atmosphere, good food and beer garden.
Blumenstrasse 5.
Tel: (089) 232 3830.
Open: daily 9am–1am.

NON-BAVARIAN FOOD IN MUNICH
American
Julep's ★
Excellent bar, solid TexMex food, good atmosphere.
Breisacher Strasse 18, Haidhausen.
Tel: (089) 448 0044.
Open: daily 5pm–1am.

Lunch at a *Wursthaus* is always a good choice

Arabian

Arabesk ★★

Belly dancing accompanies the meal, and you can exchange your filter cigarettes for a hookah.
Kaulbachstrasse 86,
Schwabing.
Tel: (089) 333 738;
www.arabesk.de.
Open: daily 6pm–1am.

French

Tantris ★★★

Gourmet restaurant with lunchtime menus beginning at around €55.
Johann-Fichte-Strasse 7.
Tel: (089) 361 9590.
Open: daily, except Mon,
noon–3pm &
6.30pm–1am.

International

Forum ★

Good breakfasts, friendly staff and good cocktails to start off the evening.
Corneliusstrasse 2.
Tel: (089) 260 8169.
Open: Sun–Wed 8am–
1am, Thur–Sat 8am–3am.

Landersdorfer &
Innerhofer ★★

Highly refined and innovative cuisine that goes beyond mere fusion.
Schloss Hackenstrasse 6–8.
Tel: (089) 2601 8637.
Open: Mon–Fri 11.30am–
2pm & 6.30pm–1am, Sat
11.30am–2pm.

Irish

Günther Murphy's ★

One of Munich's many Irish pubs with Guinness, food you can recognise, and live coverage of rugby and soccer matches.
Maistrasse 53.
Tel: (089) 534 530.

Italian

Brenner Grill Pasta
Bar ★★★

Set inside the former royal stables, Brenner Grill's tables are under vaulted arches supported by massive columns. Along with pasta dishes are fish and meat mains prepared at open grilling stations throughout the restaurant.
Maximilianstrasse 15.
Tel: (089) 452 2880;
www.brennergrill.de.
Open: until 1am
Mon–Wed, 2am
Thur–Sat.

Galleria ★★

Both the food and ambience of this Munich favourite are south-of-the-Alps, with sparkling Italian dishes such as lamb *osso buco* with *risotto* and medallions of wild boar with Shitake mushrooms.
Sparkassenstrasse 11.
Tel: (089) 297 995;
www.ristorante-
galleria.de.
Open: Mon–Sat
noon–2.30pm &
6.30pm–midnight.

Mexican

Joe Peñas Cantina ★

Another branch of the chain, found throughout Germany, serves dependable (but uninspired) tacos, burritos and fajitas when you have a TexMex craving.
Buttermelcherstrasse 17.
Tel: (089) 226 463;
www.joepenas.de.
Open: daily 5pm–1am.

Thai

Ginkao ★★

Authentic Thai cuisine in pleasant surroundings.
Morassistrasse 16.
Tel: (089) 2102 0676.
Open: Mon–Fri
11.30am–3pm &
6pm–1am. Weekends only
open evenings.

Ruen Thai ★★

With the feel of a private home and no-holds-barred spicing, Ruen Thai is worth the trip out of the city centre.
Kazmairstrasse 58,
Westend. Tel: (089) 503
239. Open: noon–2.30pm
& 6pm–midnight
Mon–Fri; 6pm–midnight
Sat–Sun.

SOUTHEAST BAVARIA

Altötting

Zur Post ★★
An attractive and extremely comfortable hotel overlooking the central square of the town and serving excellent cuisine.
Kapellenplatz 2.
Tel: (08671) 5040.

Bad Reichenhall

Hotel-Restaurant Hansi ★
Serves vegetarian dishes.
Rinckstrasse 3.
Tel: (08651) 98310;
www.hotel-hansi.de.
Open: Mon–Sat 11.30am–1pm & 6–7pm.

Steigenberger-Axelmannstein ★★
A hotel reputed for its cuisine and having two restaurants, one with a garden.
Salzburger Strasse 2.
Tel: (08651) 7770;
Garden restaurant open: daily 7–10.30am & 6.30–9pm. Axelstüberl open: daily 11.30am–midnight.

Bad Tölz

Altes Zollhaus ★
This hotel serves hearty Bavarian fare, along with vegetarian dishes.
Benediktbeurer Strasse 7.
Tel: (08041) 9749.

Open: Tue–Sat 5pm–midnight, Sun 11am–midnight.

Zum Alten Fährhaus ★★★
In fine weather you can eat outside in the terraced garden. Also a hotel.
An der Isarlust 1.
Tel: (08041) 6030.
Open: Wed–Sun 11.30am–2pm & 6pm–midnight.

Berchtesgaden

Bavaria Stub'n at Hotel Bavaria ★
Attractive hotel serving regional specialities in the restaurant.
Sunklergässchen 11.
Tel: (08652) 96610.

Chiemsee

Gasthof Zum Fischer am See ★
Regional specialities and fish fresh from the lake.
Harrasserstrasse 145.
Tel: (08051) 90760.
Open: May–Sept, daily 8am–midnight, rest of year closed Mon.

Yachthotel Chiemsee ★★
Restaurant overlooking the lake.
Harrasserstrasse 49.
Tel: (08051) 6960.
Open: daily 7am–11pm.

Landshut

Bistrorant Michaelangelo ★
Italian fare in the middle of town.
Altstadt 297.
Tel: (0871) 26261.
Open: daily 8.30am–1am.

Romantik-Hotel Fürstenhof ★★★
Attractive hotel restaurant.
Stethaimer Strasse 3.
Tel: (0871) 92550.

Prost!

*Open: daily, except
Sun, noon–2pm &
6.30–10.30pm.*

Passau
Hotel Wilder Mann ★★★
Claims to date back to
the 12th century and
offers a variety of fine
food.
*Rathausplatz. Tel: (0851)
35075. Open: daily
noon–2pm & from 6pm.*
**Die Heilig-Geist-
Stiftschenke ★★**
Atmospheric
subterranean rooms,
genial service and
prodigious portions of
traditional dishes add up
to a classic Bavarian
evening. The veal is
outstanding.
*Heilig-Geist-Gasse 4.
Tel: (0851) 2607;
www.stiftskeller-passau.de.
Open: Thur–Tue
10am–1am.*
**Wirtshaus 'Goldenes
Schiff' ★**
Regional, Italian and
vegetarian food.
*Unterer Sand 8.
Tel: (0851) 34407.
Open: daily, except Sun,
11.30am–2pm &
6pm–midnight.*

Vegetarian
Buxs ★★★
Excellent self-service
restaurant.

*Frauenstrasse 9. Tel: (089)
291 9550. Open: Mon–Fri
11am–8.30pm, Sat
11am–3.30pm.*
Prinz Myshkin ★★★
Offers dishes with an
Asian flair. Good organic
wines.
*Hackenstrasse 2.
Tel: (089) 265 596.
Open: daily 11am–
1am.*

SOUTHWEST BAVARIA
Augsburg
Bauerntanz ★
Swabian specialities to be
enjoyed.
*Bauerntanzgässchen 1.
Tel: (0821) 153 644.
Open: daily 11am–
11.30pm.*
Der Weinbäck ★
Enjoy a taste of good
local wines in historic
surroundings.
*Spitalgasse 8.
Tel: (0821) 37911.
Open: daily, except Sun,
5pm–1am.*
Feinkost Kahn ★★
Gourmet food along
with cheaper fare served
in the bistro.
*Annastrasse 16.
Tel: (0821) 312 031.
Open: daily, except Sun,
11am–3pm, Fri
6pm–midnight.
Bistro open: Mon–Wed
8am–7pm, Thur & Fri
until 8pm.*

Garmisch-
Partenkirchen
**Café Restaurant
Riessersee ★**
Situated by the lake with
views of Zugspitze.
*Tel: (08821) 95440.
Open: daily 7.30am–10pm.*
**Grand-Hotel
Sonnenbichl ★★**
The Grand-Hotel
Sonnenbichl has the
highly regarded Blauer
Salon restaurant.
*Burgstrasse 97. Tel: (08821)
7020. Open: daily noon–
2.30pm & 6pm–midnight.*

Kempten
Zum Stift ★
Decent and cheap
regional food. Zum Stift
also boasts a very pleasant
beer garden.
*Stiftsplatz 1. Tel: (0831)
22388. Closed: Mon.*

Lindau
**Hotel-Restaurant
Bayerischer Hof ★★**
Exquisitely situated.
*Seepromenade.
Tel: (08382) 9150.*

CENTRAL BAVARIA
Amberg
**Casino Altdeutsche
Stube ★★**
Restaurant with a garden.
*Schrannenplatz 8.
Tel: (09621) 22664.
Closed: Thur.*

Ansbach
Orangerie im
Hofgarten ★★
Restaurant and garden.
Promenade 33. Tel: (0981)
2170. Open: daily, except
Mon, 11am–6pm.

Dinkelsbühl
Eisenkrug ★★
Good hotel with
restaurant.
Martin-Luther-Strasse 1.
Tel: (09851) 57700.
Closed: Mon–Tue.
Goldene Rose ★
Lovely situation.
Marktplatz 4.
Tel: (09851) 57750.

Eichstätt
Domherrenhof ★
Rococo façade and
excellent food.
Domplatz 5.
Tel: (08421) 6126.
Open: daily, except Mon.

Gasthof Krone ★
Beer garden.
Domplatz 3.
Tel: (08421) 4406.

Ingolstadt
Weissbräuhaus zum
Herrnbräu ★
Good local food.
Dollstrasse 3.
Tel: (0841) 32890.
Open: Tue–Sun
9am–midnight.
Schlosslände 1.
Tel: (0841) 35150.

Nürnberg
Historische
Bratwurstküche zum
Gulden Stern ★
Dedicated to serving
Nürnberg's spicy,
finger-size pork
sausages.
Zirkelschmiedgasse 26.
Tel: (0911) 205 9288.
Closed: Sun & holidays.

Bratwursthäusle bei
St Sebald ★
Typical Nürnberg
architecture and cuisine,
including local sausages.
Rathausplatz 1.
Tel: (0911) 227 695.
Closed: Sun & holidays.

Regensburg
Bishofshof am Dom ★★
The hotel's gourmet
restaurant 'David' is in
the historic Goliath
House, at Watmarkt 5.
Tel: (0941) 58460.
Open: Tue–Sat
6pm–midnight.
Historische
Wurstküche ★★
This 850-year-old
restaurant (first
mentioned in
historical records in
1615) at the foot of the
Stone Bridge is famous
for its sausages and

An open-air feast

When weather permits, dining outdoors is preferred

sauerkraut and is a major tourist attraction. Summer dining outdoors.
Steinerne Brücke, Thundorferstrasse 3.
Tel: (0941) 466 210.
Open: daily 9am–7pm.

Rothenburg ob der Tauber
Eisenhut ★★★
Quality food in a 16th-century hotel.
Herrengasse 3–5.
Tel: (09861) 7050.
Goldener Hirsch ★★
The Goldener Hirsch has fine views from the patio.
Untere Schmiedgasse 16.
Tel: (09861) 7080.
Molkerei ★
Internationally flavoured cuisine.
Schweinsdorfer Strasse 25b.
Tel: (09861) 933 310. Open:
Wed–Sun 11am–1am.

NORTHERN BAVARIA
Aschaffenburg
Hofgut Fasanerie ★
Set in a park, with a beer garden.
Bismarckallee 1.
Tel: (06021) 371 522.
Open: Wed–Sat 5pm–1am,
Sun 11.30am–1am.

Omas Kochtopf ★
Franconian and Bavarian specialities.
Löherstrasse 27.
Tel: (06021) 27625.
Open: daily 11am–2pm &
6pm–midnight.

Bamberg
Café Abseits ★
The oldest student café in Bamberg with 30 different beers (a different one served each month) and a beer garden.
Pödeldorfer Strasse 39.
Tel: (0951) 303 422.
Open: daily 9am–1am.

St Nepomuk ★
Set in a former mill.
Also a hotel.
Obere Mühlbrücke 9.
Tel: (0951) 98420. Open:
daily noon–midnight.

Coburg
Blankenburg ★
Gourmet food in the
Kräutergarten restaurant,
more down-to-earth fare
in Die Petersilie.
Rosenauer Strasse 30.
Tel: (09561) 426 080.
Open: daily
11.30am–midnight.
Coburger Tor ★★★
An excellent hotel
restaurant.
Ketschendorferstrasse 22.
Tel: (09561) 25074.
Open: daily, except Sun,
6pm–midnight.

Würzburg
Bürgerspital-
Weinstuben ★
The local wines are served
with *meefischli*, tiny fried
river fish.
Theaterstrasse 19.
Tel: (0931) 352 880.
Open: daily 9am–
midnight.
Juliusspital ★
A 16th-century alms-
house with cellars.
Juliuspromenade 19.
Tel: (0931) 54080.
Open: daily 10am–
midnight.

Riemenschneider
Weinstuben ★
Good Franconian cook-
ing and wines.
Franziskanergasse.
Tel: (0931) 571 487.
Open: Mon–Sat from
3pm, Sun from 11am.
Closed: Tue.
Weinhaus zum
Stachel ★★
Traditional fish dishes.
Gressengasse 1. Tel: (0931)
52770. Open: Mon–Sat
11am–1am.

DRINK
Tradition asserts that
Bavaria's first brewery
was set up in 724 by the
missionary St Korbinian.
Certainly, Bavarian
monks were brewing beer
in the early 14th century,
and their legacy lingers
on in *Starkbier* (strong
beer), brewed in March
and originally intended to
succour the religious
during the stringent days
of Lent.

With such a long
history of brewing, it is no
wonder that Bavaria offers
the beer drinker a broad
choice of excellent brews.
At the lighter end of the
scale are *Helles* (a term for
any pale beer, but usually
a lager), *Radler* (shandy –
Helles mixed with
lemonade), and two sorts
of *Weizenbier* (wheat beer,
also known as *Weissbier*)
– *Hefeweizen* and
Kristallweizen (the latter
is the filtered version and
is usually served with a
slice of lemon in it).
Stronger beer types are
Bock, *Doppelbock* (double
strength) and *Starkbier*;
Dunkel/Dunkles is any
dark beer. Others worth
trying are *Rauchbier*
(smoked beer) and
Märzen (a speciality of
the Oktoberfest). Draught
beer is known as *vom Fass*
and is a hoppy lager.
Bavaria's brewing
industry is still regulated

Although beer is Bavaria's favourite beverage, there are some
celebrated wines as well

Careful balancing act

by principles laid down by Duke Wilhelm IV in 1516, who limited the ingredients to yeast, barley, hops and water.

Munich's major beers are Hofbräu, Löwenbräu, Hackerbräu, Pschorrbräu, Spatenbräu, Paulaner-Thomasbräu and Augustinerbräu. In the city's beer cellars and gardens skilled waitresses will carry half-a-dozen or more glasses or ceramic jugs, each foaming with a litre of beer.

The beergarden is a way of life in Bavaria. You can talk to people you would probably not meet elsewhere, or you can simply sit under the trees, alone with your thoughts, listening to music and the hum of animated conversation.

Beer cellars and gardens

The following are among Munich's beer cellars and gardens:

Augustinerkeller
Selling the high-quality Augustiner beer, the cellar also serves traditional Bavarian food.
Arnulfstrasse 52.
Tel: (089) 594 393.
Open: daily 10.30am–midnight.

Aumeister
At the northern end of the Englischer Garten, and more tranquil than the busy Chinese Pagoda garden. A great place to escape the noise and hectic bustle of the big city. Take the U6 to Freimann.
Sondermeierstrasse 1.
Tel: (089) 325 224.
Open: daily, except Mon, 9am–11pm.

Biergarten am Chinesischen Turm
The popular 'Beer garden by the Chinese Pagoda' has a seating capacity of up to 7,000, making this Munich's largest beer garden.
Englischer Garten 3.
Tel: (089) 383 8730.
Open: daily 10am–midnight.

Hirschgarten
Families with children are particularly welcome.
Hirschgartenallee 1.
Tel: (089) 172 591.
Open: daily 10am–midnight.

Hofbräuhaus
The most famous beer cellar in Germany.
Am Platzl 9. Tel: (089) 221 676. Open: daily 9am–midnight.

Löwenbräukeller
The main outlet for one of the city's celebrated breweries.
Nymphenburgerstrasse 2.
Tel: (089) 526 021.
Open: daily 9am–midnight.

Seehaus
Beautifully situated next to a lake in the Englischer Garten, with majestic old trees providing shade in summer. Not all that far away is Hirschau (*tel: (089) 369 945*), another

good beer garden at Gysslingstrasse 15. *Kleinhesselohe 2. Tel: (089) 381 6130. Open: daily 10am–midnight.*

Waldwirtschaft Grosshesselohe

Up to 2,000 revellers can sit down to drink here. *Georg-Kalb-Strasse 3. Tel: (089) 7499 4030. Open: Mon–Sat 11am–9pm, Sun to 8pm.*

Wine and wine bars

The wines of Bavaria are cultivated in Franconia, in the easternmost vineyards of western Germany, centring on Würzburg. Grapes are grown on the slopes of the River Main and its tributaries, the main varieties being Silvaner and Müller-Thurgau. In former times, these wines were all given the name *Steinwein*, named after a celebrated Würzburg vineyard. They are bottled in a green, squat flagon known as a *Bocksbeutel*.

Würzburg (*see p126*) remains the major centre for sampling Franconian wines. Its most celebrated *Weinstuben* (wine bars) can be visited in the Bürgerspital (*see p131*), established in the 14th century to shelter the aged and still doing so, funded by the sale of wines from its own vineyards (*Theaterstrasse 19; tel: (0931) 352 880*).

Other good wine bars are the WeinGasthof im Haus des Frankenweins (*Kranenkai 1; tel: (0931) 50130; open: daily 11am–11pm*), which also boasts a lovely garden to wine and dine in, and the Juliusspital-Weinstuben (*Juliuspromenade 19; tel: (0931) 54080*).

Naturally Munich also has its *Weinstuben*, among them the Pfälzer Weinprobierstube in the Residenz (*Residenzstrasse 1; tel: (089) 225 628; open: daily 10am–11.30pm*); the vaulted Weinstadl (*Burgstrasse 5; tel: (089) 2280 7420; open: daily 11.30am–midnight*); and the Weinhaus Neuner (*Herzogspitalstrasse 8; tel: (089) 260 3954; open: Mon–Sat 11.30am–3pm & 5.30pm–midnight*). Munich's oldest wine bar, it celebrated its 150th jubilee in 2002.

Food and drink, the company of friends – a café bar in Munich

Hotels and accommodation

Bavaria receives about one-third of all the German holidaymakers who choose to stay at home for their holiday, not to mention an equal number of travellers from abroad. As a result, the total number of nights spent each year in hotels and private accommodation amounts to a staggering 74 million. To cope, the region has some 500,000 beds available in hotels and private houses.

A traditional Bavarian Gasthaus (inn)

Munich alone has some 350 hotels and guesthouses with over 40,000 beds. Despite this, hotels and guesthouses are rarely likely to have empty rooms during the festive season or the main summer holiday period, and advance booking is necessary.

The choice is wide. Double rooms in de luxe hotels, such as the celebrated Vier Jahreszeiten in Maximilianstrasse, Munich, start at around €380. In a medium-price hotel double rooms start at €110. Always enquire about special offers. Even plush hotels sometimes offer short-break packages of three nights with bed and breakfast for as little as €150, and weekends with full board for around €120.

Rooms are usually cheaper outside the capital (the exception being popular tourist spots such as Oberammergau). In most villages, a *Gasthof* will be surprisingly inexpensive. The sign *Zimmer frei* indicates bed and breakfast.

Rural Bavaria has many a fine country inn, often with a long history of serving travellers. A bewildering series of names depicts such hostelries: *Gasthof*,

Gasthaus, Gästehaus, Pension, Hotel, while *Ferien-wohnungen* are self-catering holiday apartments. The cheaper hotels generally offer hot and cold water in your room, with shared shower or bathroom facilities.

If you are exploring the country without an advance booking, make sure you start looking early enough for a bed for the night, certainly before 6pm, when inns start serving evening meals. Remember, innkeepers usually take a day off during the week (the *Ruhetag*), when you may still be able to book a room, but the restaurant will be closed.

Invariably, it is safer to book ahead, especially in holiday season. Tourist offices all have lists of hotels, many of which can be viewed and booked online. Many tourist offices are happy to find and book accommodation for visitors on the spot; when you write, specify the price category, the kind of rooms you require and your exact holiday dates.

Ambience

Many inns, especially those in small villages, preserve such traditional features as the old and beautifully tiled stove (the *Kachelofen*), even though every room is nowadays centrally heated. If the inn is attached to a pig farm, the pork chops will be unusually succulent (look for the sign *Hausschlachtung/Metzgerei*, meaning 'home butchery').

In almost every hotel and restaurant, you find the traditional host's table, the *Stammtisch*. Invariably, it lacks a table cloth, though the *Stammtisch* will usually be a far more elaborate and intricately carved affair than the other tables in the inn. Often a finely wrought metal ornament declares its name. Casual guests at the inn do not sit here. Instead, towards the end of an evening, the host, having checked with each guest that all is well with the meal, will sit with his friends, often playing cards.

Hotel services

Animals are welcome at hotels with the slogan *Haustiere willkommen* ('Pets welcome'), and you can take dogs to hotels that say *Hundefreundlich*. Nearly all hotels have direct-dial telephones in their rooms. Increasingly, hotels have no-smoking rooms (*Nichtraucherzimmer*). Some also offer menus to cater for special diets (*Diätkost auf Wunsch*). On a family holiday, you can ask for an additional bed to be provided in your room (*Zusatzbett möglich*).

Alpine huts

Climbers and mountain hikers can double their pleasure by spending a night on the summit, watching the sun go down, and waking at dawn to witness the sun rising again. The Berchtes-

gadener Land, in particular, specialises in so-called Alpine huts which, though facilities vary, are far more comfortable than the name implies. Detailed information can be obtained from the Berchtesgaden tourist office (*83741 Berchtesgaden; tel: (08652) 9670*).

Münchener Schlüssel (Munich Key)

Offered by the Munich tourist office, this weekend accommodation package includes reductions on the city's attractions, a pass for the city's transport system, as well as a hotel booking. For details contact a travel agent or visit the Munich tourist office online.

Online hotel bookings

Where a tourist office provides an English language website, it is listed next to the address in the main text. There are also central online booking services available on the internet (focused on the more upmarket establishments):
www.deutschland-hotel.de
(good for Munich and environs);
www.nethotels.com and
www.hotelstravel.com/germany-ba.html
(for all Bavaria);
www.munich.nethotels.com
(for Munich);
www.german-romantic-hotels.com
(for historic and castle hotels throughout Germany, but also some in Bavaria);
www.hotel-reservation-germany.com
(hotel bookings throughout Germany);
www.bayern-hotel.de/e/karte.phtml
(hotels in Bavaria, in German);
www.bayerngastronom.de/eindex.html
(hotels, bed & breakfasts and restaurants in Bavaria, in German).

On business

One of Gemany's richest states, Bavaria has an export economy the size of those of Switzerland and Sweden. Its principal exports are motor vehicles, followed by machinery, electrical goods and chemical products. Electrical goods, vehicles, machinery and chemical products also figure among the state's chief imports, as well as agricultural products, beer, food and clothing.

The landmark BMW building

Banking
Bavaria boasts more banks than any other German state. The largest bank, the Bayerisches Landesbank Girozentrale, is half owned by the Free State itself and half by the savings banks. After Frankfurt, Munich is the largest banking centre in Germany.

Business entertaining
Most entertaining takes place in a hotel or restaurant. It is rare to be invited into someone's home for a business meal, but where this does happen (generally for an evening meal) arrive spot on time and, as an added courtesy, bring a bouquet of flowers. If there are children in the family, inexpensive presents for them are also appreciated. The meal begins with the phrase *Guten Appetit*, while 'your health' in German is either *Zum Wohl* or *Prosit*. In spite of the fact that Bavarians, like all Germans, are happy to begin work early, expect also to stay fairly late.

Business etiquette
English is a compulsory subject in German schools, with the consequence that your German business colleague will certainly speak it. Nonetheless, it is appreciated if any sales literature you may wish to hand out is in German.

Even more important is punctuality. Bavarians start work as early as 7am. There is no fixed time for lunch, which usually takes no more than half an hour. Dress, too, is important; Bavarian businessmen and women dress smartly and regard this as a sign of professionalism.

As a matter of natural courtesy, you will be expected to shake hands (with all the people present) at the beginning and at the end of a business meeting, the most senior person usually offering a hand first. Equally, the custom is never to address people by their Christian name unless you are requested to. Usually you would address them formally (Frau Dr Rumpler; Herr Direktor, and so on).

Chambers of Industry and Commerce
An invaluable source of information and help, the Deutsche Industrie-und-Handelskammer for Munich and Upper Bavaria is located at *Max-Joseph-Strasse 2, 80323 München; tel: (089) 51160;*

e-mail: ihkmail@muenchen.ihk.de).
Other Chambers of Industry and
Commerce can be found throughout
Bavaria. Among the more important are:
Aschaffenburg, *Kerschensteinerstrasse 9
(tel: (06021) 8800; e-mail:
ihk@aschaffenburg.ihk.de)*; **Augsburg**,
Stettenstrasse 1 and 3 (tel: (0821) 31621);
Bayreuth, *Bahnhofstrasse 25–27
(tel: (0921) 8860; e-mail:
ihk.bt@bayreuth.ihk.de)*; **Coburg**,
*Schlossplatz 5 (tel: (09561) 74260;
e-mail: ihk@coburg.ihk.de)*; **Lindau-
Bodensee**, *Uferweg 9 (tel: (08382) 93830;
e-mail: ihk@lindau.ihk.de)*; **Nürnberg**,
*Hauptmarkt 25–27 (tel: (0911) 13350;
fax: (0911) 133 5200)*; **Passau**,
*Nibelungstrasse 15 (tel: (0851) 5070;
e-mail: ihk@passau.ihk.de)*; **Regensburg**,
*Dr-Martin-Luther-Strasse 12 (tel: (0941)
56940; e-mail: info@regensburg.ihk.de)*;
and **Würzburg**, *Mainaustrasse 33
(tel: (0931) 41940; fax: (0931) 419 4100)*.

Conference centres

All the big hotels in Bavaria have
conference centres, fully equipped with
state-of-the-art technology, often also
offering secretarial and translation
facilities. Augsburg has a trade-fair
centre, the Schwabenhallen, which can
accommodate up to 1,200 *(tel: (0821)
25720; www.messeaugsburg.de)*, as well as
a congress hall in the Wittelsbacher
Park, linked to Europe's highest tower
hotel *(tel: (0821) 324 2348)*. The city
information office *(tel: (0821) 502 070)*
publishes a guide (in English and
German) entirely devoted to trade fairs
and congresses.

Bamberg has imaginatively
transformed several historical buildings

into conference centres. Modern,
purpose-built facilities include those
offered by Forum Bamberg *(tel: (0951)
917 7100; e-mail: info@Forum-
Bamberg.com)*, and the city's Congress
Hall *(tel: (0951) 964 7200; e-mail:
info@konzerthalle-bamberg.de)*. Coburg's
Kongresshaus Rosengarten in Berliner
Platz *(tel: (09561) 74180)* has ten
conference rooms (the largest, the
Festsaal, accommodating up to 1,100),
with a total of 16 variable room
combinations. Conference organisers are
also provided with personal offices.

Munich boasts the massive
Messegelände complex *(tel: (089) 9492
0720; www.messe-muenchen.de)*. The city
plays host to approximately 1,000 major
congresses, conventions and seminars a
year.

Nürnberg actively promotes itself as a
conference city, and the tourist board
has a special department dealing with
enquiries *(tel: (0911) 23360)*, while
nearby Fürth and Erlangen have equally
well-equipped conference centres.

For conferences in Regensburg, you
can book, among others, the
Dollingersaal of the Altes Rathaus, or
the recently renovated Neuhaus-Saal
(for all conference halls belonging to the
city, *tel: (0941) 507 1415)*. The city hosts
a biennial trade fair in March/April
specialising in consumer goods
produced in eastern Bavaria.

Würzburg calls itself a 'Congress City'.
The Congress Centrum Würzburg can
seat around 1,600, the historic
Barockhäuser seats 100 (for both these
centres, *tel: (0931) 372 372)*, and the
Tagungszentrum Hofstuben seats some
400 people *(tel: (0931) 47091)*.

Practical guide

Arriving
Entry regulations
Visitors from European Union countries, the USA, Australia, Canada, Switzerland and New Zealand need only a valid passport to stay for up to three months. Some other nationals also need a visa – check beforehand at German embassies or consulates.

By air
Bavaria has two international airports, a small one at Nürnberg and a major one at Munich, as well as many commercial ones. International airlines operate scheduled services to Munich, while the German national airline, Lufthansa, serves both Munich and Nürnberg from major international cities. easyJet flies to Munich from airports all over the UK and continental Europe, often at better-than-bargain rates.

U-Bahn 2 runs roughly every 10 minutes from the main railway station (Hauptbahnhof) to Nürnberg airport. The ride takes about 12 minutes. For flight information you can *tel: (0911) 93700*, or view the website at *www.airport-nuernberg.de*

Taxis to Munich's main railway station are expensive. The airport express bus (running every 20 minutes) is much cheaper. However, this may not be the best alternative as the journey can take anywhere between 30 minutes and three hours, depending on the traffic.

The most reliable form of transport (taking around 40 minutes) is the S-Bahn 8, with trains running every 10 minutes between the airport and the main railway station. For flight information *tel: (089) 9752 1313*.

By car
Motorways run from the main ferry ports in northern France, Belgium, the Netherlands and Germany, reaching northern Bavaria via Heilsbronn, central Bavaria via Augsburg and southern Bavaria via Ulm. Munich is 850km (528 miles) from Ostend and 995km (618 miles) from both Calais and Boulogne; 960km (597 miles) from Dunkirk, 875km (544 miles) from the Hook of Holland and 890km (553 miles) from Vlissingen.

By train
Trains (with couchettes and sleepers) take 18 hours to reach Munich from Calais or Ostend. French Railways (SNCF) operate a motorail service from Paris to Munich, taking around 10 hours.

Camping
German campsites are uniformly excellent. Apply for information to the Deutscher Camping Club, *Mandlstrasse 28, Munich 80802 (tel: (089) 380 1420)*. In summer, many of the best sites are soon full, so it is always better to book ahead, if possible. Owners of campsites are not required to insure campers for losses or theft.

Children
Children are made a great deal of in Bavaria, and you can expect to be the centre of attention if your children are well behaved.

Climate

In summer visitors can expect bright skies and warm weather that is rarely so hot as to be unbearable, but be prepared for cloudy and wet days. Snowfall is common in winter (*see also p18*) so best come prepared.

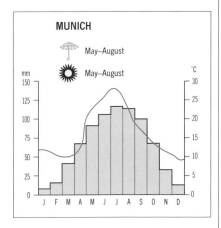

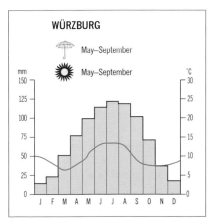

Weather Conversion Chart
25.4mm = 1 inch
°F = 1.8 x °C + 32

Conversion tables

See p183.
Clothes and shoe sizes in Bavaria follow the standard sizes used in the rest of Europe.

Crime

Don't leave purses, wallets, cameras and other valuables in places where they can be stolen easily – in cars or back pockets.

Customs regulations

There is no limit to the quantity of goods that you can take in or out of Germany so long as they were purchased in another EU state. There are restrictions on goods purchased free of customs duty and VAT in duty-free shops. These limits are clearly signposted. Similar limits apply to alcohol, tobacco and certain cosmetic products imported from outside the European Union.

Cyclists

Munich's Allgemeiner Deutscher Fahrradclub (*ADFC, Platenstrasse 4; tel: (089) 773 429*) publishes maps showing cycle routes. The Munich tourist office also provides information on cycle tours of the city. Bicycles can be hired at many Bavarian railway stations. Express trains ban cycles, but they can be carried on public transport and on normal trains, so long as you buy a bicycle ticket (*Fahrradkarte*).

Driving

Be careful to stay in the right-hand lane except when overtaking. Outside built-up areas cars ought, by law, to travel at no more than 100kph (62mph), while in built-up areas the speed limit is 50kph (31mph). Cars with trailers are limited to 80kph (50mph) on main roads and motorways. There is no speed limit on motorways (though a top speed of 130kph (81mph) is recommended). Drunken drivers face severe punishment.

At crossroads and roundabouts, unless otherwise indicated by road signs, traffic from the right has priority. Most pedestrian crossings in the cities have traffic lights which must be obeyed. Wear seatbelts in the rear and front seats. Children under 12 may not travel in the front seats of cars.

Breakdown
Germany's automobile association, the ADAC (*Allgemeiner Deutscher Automobil-Club, Am Westpark 8, Munich 81373; tel: (089) 767 676; Nürnberg tel: (0911) 208 004*) provides emergency assistance free of charge for members of affiliated clubs (you pay for any parts that need replacing). For the ADAC breakdown service (24 hours) *tel: 0180 222 2222.*

Documents
To drive in Bavaria you need a valid EU (pink) driving licence; you can also drive on a non-EU licence but you must carry a German translation (available at consulates and motoring organisations).

Insurance
If you hire a car, collision insurance, often called collision damage waiver or CDW, is normally offered by the hirer, and is usually compulsory. Check with

your own motor insurers before you leave, as you may be covered by your normal policy. If not, CDW is payable locally and may be as much as 50 per cent of the hiring fee. Neither CDW nor your personal travel insurance will protect you for liability arising out of an accident in a hired car, for instance if you damage another vehicle or injure someone. If you are likely to hire a car, you should obtain such extra cover, preferably from your travel agent or other insurer before departure.

If you are taking your own motor vehicle on holiday, check with your motoring insurers on your cover for damage, loss, theft of the vehicle, and for liability. A Green Card is recommended. It is also possible to buy extra cover for expenses resulting from breakdowns and accidents.

Electricity
220 volts; two-pin sockets.

Embassies and consulates in Munich
Canada *Am Thal 29.*
Tel: (089) 219 9570.
Ireland *Denninger Strasse 15.*
Tel: (089) 2080 5990.
UK *Bürkleinstrasse 10.*
Tel: (089) 211 090.
USA *Königinstrasse 5. Tel: (089) 28880.*

Emergency telephone numbers
Police *110*
Fire *112*
Ambulance *112*
Medical Aid *551 771*
MasterCard/Eurocard loss or theft *(069) 7933 1910; 001 314 275 6690* (International).

Health

European tick-borne encephalitis is the most serious recognised arboviral illness in Europe. In forested areas, it is advisable to wear long-sleeved clothing, no shorts or sandals, and use insect repellents. Avoid unpasteurised cow, goat and sheep milk products. If bitten by a tick, consult a local physician immediately.

Residents of EU nations should carry their European Health Insurance Card (EHIC), available from *www.ehic.org.uk*, by phoning *0845 606 2030* or from post offices. This covers any publicly provided medical treatment in Germany, unless medical treatment is the primary reason for being there. Non EU nationals are also covered, but it is a good practice to carry travellers' insurance with medical transport included.

The cost of prescribed medicines bought from a chemist is not recoverable. If you need hospital treatment the local insurance office will give you a certificate (a *Kostenübernahmeschein*) to present to the hospital authorities. If you need urgent hospital treatment, show the secretariat your card and the hospital will get the certificate on your behalf.

Hitch-hiking

Strictly forbidden on the motorways themselves, hitch-hiking is permitted at motorway entrances (as far as the blue sign with the white motorway logo). Students can arrange a lift in advance by consulting the bulletin boards at the university *Mensas* (eating places open to any student with a valid student card).

Conversion Table

FROM	TO	MULTIPLY BY
Inches	Centimetres	2.54
Feet	Metres	0.3048
Yards	Metres	0.9144
Miles	Kilometres	1.6090
Acres	Hectares	0.4047
Gallons	Litres	4.5460
Ounces	Grams	28.35
Pounds	Grams	453.6
Pounds	Kilograms	0.4536
Tons	Tonnes	1.0160

To convert back, for example from centimetres to inches, divide by the number in the third column.

Men's Suits

UK	36	38	40	42	44	46	48
Rest of Europe	46	48	50	52	54	56	58
USA	36	38	40	42	44	46	48

Dress Sizes

UK	8	10	12	14	16	18
France	36	38	40	42	44	46
Italy	38	40	42	44	46	48
Rest of Europe	34	36	38	40	42	44
USA	6	8	10	12	14	16

Men's Shirts

UK	14	14.5	15	15.5	16	16.5	17
Rest of Europe	36	37	38	39/40	41	42	43
USA	14	14.5	15	15.5	16	16.5	17

Men's Shoes

UK	7	7.5	8.5	9.5	10.5	11
Rest of Europe	41	42	43	44	45	46
USA	8	8.5	9.5	10.5	11.5	12

Women's Shoes

UK	4.5	5	5.5	6	6.5	7
Rest of Europe	38	38	39	39	40	41
USA	6	6.5	7	7.5	8	8.5

Insurance

You should take out personal travel insurance before leaving, from your travel agent, tour operator or insurance company. It should give adequate cover for medical expenses, loss and theft, personal liability (but liability arising from motor accidents is not usually covered – *see p182*) and cancellation expenses. Always read the conditions, any exclusions, and details of cover, and check that the amount of cover is adequate.

Lost property

The lost property office in Munich is at *Oetztaler Strasse 17 (tel: (089) 23300)*. For property lost on railway trains or in stations, you should contact the Fundstelle der Bundesbahn, Munich Hauptbahnhof (main station), *Bahnhofplatz 2, opposite platform 26 (tel: (089) 1308 6664)*.

Maps

All tourist offices provide free maps of local cities and towns, though for more detailed maps you must pay a small charge. For hiking, cycling or climbing, many bookshops offer a relatively inexpensive *Wanderkarte* (map with walking routes).

Media
Press

Bavaria's leading daily paper is the *Süddeutsche Zeitung*, published in Munich, which is full of useful information and which carries a listings section every day covering all the main events, with a bumper edition on Friday. *Munich Found*, Bavaria's city magazine

in English, is available from most Munich newsagents. The online version is available at the following address: *www.munichfound.de*

Television

Bavaria has over 20 channels. CNN news in English is usually available at hotels with cable or satellite connections.

Money matters

Traveller's cheques are accepted in hotels and larger restaurants but in very few shops. The same is true of credit cards; most Bavarians prefer cash. Traveller's cheques and foreign currency can be changed at all post offices and at most banks. Ask whether there is a minimum charge before changing, since this can be a disproportionate amount if you only want to change small sums.

National holidays

1 January New Year's Day
6 January Epiphany
End Feb/early Mar Shrove Tuesday
Variable Good Friday
Variable Easter Monday
1 May Labour Day
Variable Ascension Day
Variable Whit Monday
Variable Corpus Christi
15 August Assumption
3 October Unification Day
1 November All Saints' Day
24, 25 & 26 December Christmas

Opening hours

In the (inner) cities shops are open Monday to Friday 9/10am–8pm and Saturday to 4pm. Elsewhere, shops tend

LANGUAGE

Although many Bavarians have a reasonable command of English, you will find the following words and phrases useful.

BASIC WORDS AND PHRASES

hello	Grüss Gott
	(far more common in Bavaria than the usual German 'guten Tag')
goodbye	auf Wiedersehen
good morning	guten Morgen
good evening	guten Abend
please	bitte
many thanks	danke schön
yes	ja
no	nein
left	links
right	rechts
warm	warm
cold	kalt
large	gross
small	klein
cheap	billig
expensive	teuer
open	offen
closed	geschlossen
Do you speak English?	Sprechen Sie Englisch?
I do not understand	Ich verstehe nicht

NUMBERS

1	eins	7	sieben
2	zwei /zwo	8	acht
3	drei	9	neun
4	vier	10	zehn
5	fünf	11	elf
6	sechs	12	zwölf

DAYS OF THE WEEK

Sunday	Sonntag
Monday	Montag
Tuesday	Dienstag
Wednesday	Mittwoch
Thursday	Donnerstag
Friday	Freitag
Saturday	Samstag
	(or Sonnabend)

MONTHS OF THE YEAR

January	Januar
February	Februar
March	März
April	April
May	Mai
June	Juni
July	Juli
August	August
September	September
October	Oktober
November	November
December	Dezember

HOTELS

I should like	Ich möchte
bathroom	Badezimmer
double room	Doppelzimmer
single room	Einzelzimmer
breakfast	Frühstück
how much?	Was kostet?

HOTEL-RESERVATION

to open Monday to Friday 8/9am–6pm, often closing for lunch; Saturdays until noon or 1pm. However, even in smaller towns, large supermarkets and stores may stay open longer during the week (to 8pm) and on Saturdays (to 4pm). Bakeries always open early, around 7am, and some may open on Sunday mornings. (*Also see p19.*)

Pharmacies
English-speaking pharmacists can be consulted at Bahnhof Apotheke, 2 Bahnhofplatz (*tel: (089) 594 119*) by Munich railway station.

Police
In an emergency, telephone *110*. Otherwise seek help from the nearest police station.

Post offices
You will usually find the main post office – the Hauptpostamt – near the railway station in any town. You can buy stamps in newsagents and souvenir shops.

Public transport
In Munich, U-Bahn (underground) services are the fastest way of getting around the city centre, and S-Bahn (suburban line trains) provides services to within a 40-km (25-mile) radius of the city centre. Most other cities in Bavaria have good bus and tram networks.

Student and youth travel
Munich has a good number of young people's guesthouses, such as the Haus International, *Elisabethstrasse 87 (tel: (089) 120 060). The main youth hostel (Jugendherberge) is at Wendl-Dietrich-Strasse 20 (tel: (089) 131 156). Other hostels include Euro Youth Hotel, Senefelderstrasse 5 (tel: 089 5990 8811), 4 You München, Hirtenstrasse 18 (tel: (089) 552 1660) and IN VIA Marienherberge (for girls up to 25 only), Goethestrasse 9 (tel: (089) 555 805).*

Teenagers, and anybody up to the age of 25, can get 20 per cent reductions on long-distance rail travel in second-class compartments with the TwenTicket. The ticket is valid for either a single (*einfach*) or return (*hin und zurück*) journey. The Bayern-Ticket (no age

A Communicarta
Style 45 design
© Communicarta Ltd 2006 UDN.4b
Map user Ref:WZFG/TVL/MUC/2006/50/4

U-Bahn and S-Bahn

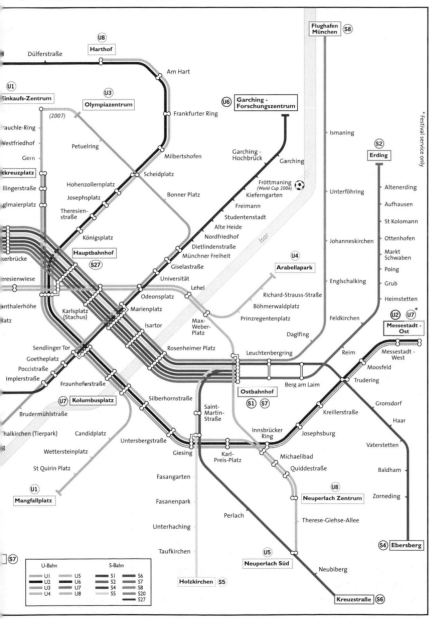

limitation) allows unlimited travel
on trains for up to five people for one
day throughout Bavaria. More details
and information on other discount
tickets are available from information
counters at main railway stations or at
www.bahn.de

Sustainable tourism
Thomas Cook is a strong advocate of
ethical and fairly traded tourism and
believes that the travel experience
should be as good for the places visited
as it is for the people who visit them.
That's why we firmly support The
Travel Foundation, a charity that
develops solutions to help improve and
protect holiday destinations, their
environment, traditions and culture.
To find out what you can do to make
a positive difference to the places
you travel to and the people who live
there, please visit
www.thetravelfoundation.org.uk

Telephones
Make international calls from boxes
marked *Inland und Auslandgesprache.*
The international access code is *00.*
Country codes:
Australia *61*
Canada *1*
Ireland *353*
New Zealand *64*
UK *44*
USA *1*

Time
Bavaria observes Continental European
Time which is one hour ahead of
Greenwich Mean Time (GMT) in winter
and two hours ahead in summer.

Tipping
Though service charges are added to the
bill, leave the small coins in your change.
A tip of 5 to 10 per cent is the norm.

Toilets
Toiletten are marked *Damen* (women)
and *Herren* (men). Often there is a
small charge.

Tourist offices
Canada German National Tourist
Office, *480 University Avenue, Suite 1410,
Toronto, Ontario M5G 1V2. Tel: (001)
416 968 1685; fax: (001) 416 968 0562.*
UK German National Tourist Office,
*PO Box 2695, London W1A 3TN
(tel: (020) 7317 0908).*
USA German National Tourist Office,
*122 East 42nd Street, Suite 2000, New
York, NY 10168-0072 (tel: (212) 661
7200; www.cometogermany.com);*
German National Tourist Office,
*1334 Parkview Avenue, Suite 300,
Manhattan Beach, CA 90266. Tel: (001)
310 545 1350; fax: (001) 310 545 1371.*

Travellers with disabilities
The German National Tourist Offices
will supply hotel lists indicating special
facilities for travellers with disabilities.
The central German organisation for
people with disabilities is Hilfe für
Behinderte, *Kirchfeldstrasse 149, 40215
Düsseldorf; tel: (0211) 310 060; e-mail:
info@bagh.de.* For the blind, the
Bayerischer Blinden-und
Sehbehindertenbund EV (*e-mail:
muenchen@bbsb.org*) in Munich is at
Arnulfstrasse 22 (*near the main railway
station; open: Mon, Wed & Fri
9am–noon, Tue & Thur 4–6pm*).

ACKNOWLEDGEMENTS

Thomas Cook Publishing wishes to thank the following photographers, libraries and associations, for their assistance in the preparation of this book, to whom the copyright in the photographs belongs:

www.bigfoto.com 119
LANDESHAUPTSTADT MÜNCHEN TOURISMUSAMT 22, 28, 59 (Wilfried Hoesl), 146, 150, 175
PICTURES COLOUR LIBRARY 33, 44b, 91a, 91b, 159
SPECTRUM COLOUR LIBRARY 1, 29b, 40, 45, 49, 90, 128, 147, 148a, 156b, 157b, 158a, 158b, 171, 178
STILLMAN ROGERS 2, 10, 15, 21, 27, 35, 37, 65, 140, 141, 142, 143, 145, 151, 155, 156a, 163, 167, 169, 172
THE THOMAS COOK ARCHIVE 18
LANDESTHEATER COBURG 152
TOURIST INFORMATION OFFICE, NORDLINGEN 102
WORLD PICTURES 61, 64

The remaining pictures are held in the AA PHOTO LIBRARY and were taken by: ANTONY SOUTER with the exception of pages 6, 13b, 13c, 17, 69, 70, 73, 82, 86, 87, 101, 103, 104, 105, 106, 107, 108, 109, 111, 113, 116, 117, 121, 129a, 135, 137, 144 which were taken by ADRIAN BAKER.

Index: MARIE LORIMER
Proofreading: JAN McCANN for CAMBRIDGE PUBLISHING MANAGEMENT LIMITED

Send your thoughts to
books@thomascook.com

We're committed to providing the very best up-to-date information in our travel guides and constantly strive to make them as useful as they can be. You can help us to improve future editions by letting us have your feedback. If you've made a wonderful discovery on your travels that we don't already feature, if you'd like to inform us about recent changes to anything that we do include, or if you simply want to let us know your thoughts about this guidebook and how we can make it even better – we'd love to hear from you.

Send us ideas, discoveries and recommendations today and then look out for your valuable input in the next edition of this title. And, as an extra 'thank you' from Thomas Cook Publishing, you'll be automatically entered into our exciting monthly prize draw.

Emails to the above address, or letters to Travellers Project Editor, Thomas Cook Publishing, PO Box 227, Unit 18, Coningsby Road, Peterborough PE3 8SB, UK.

Please don't forget to let us know which title your feedback refers to!